PSYCHIC SCOTLAND

PSYCHIC SCOTLAND

Tom Rannachan

Black & White Publishing

First published 2007
by Black & White Publishing Ltd
99 Giles Street, Edinburgh EH6 6BZ

1 3 5 7 9 10 8 6 4 2 07 08 09 10 11

ISBN 13: 978 1 84502 182 5
ISBN 10: 1 84502 182 7

Typeset by GreenGate Publishing Services, Tonbridge, Kent
Printed and bound by Creative Print and Design Group Ltd

ACKNOWLEDGEMENTS

Special thanks to Lorraine Kenyon, animal communicator, and Alex from Paranormal Investigation Scotland for their input. It's highly appreciated.

Thanks to Thomas Murphy, Marie Docherty, Scott and Joanne MacDougall, Catherine and Scott Nicholls, Anne Marie and Gerry Hart, Robert and Nina Law, Louise Law and Tommy Hughes, the McAlpine family, Rose and Ian McNeil, the Tinto family, Maggie and Andy Carson, John and Michelle Perry and family, Marie McNaughton, Guy Ramsay, Alan Walker, Uncle Billy and Karen, Iain McArthur, Gavin Joyce, Derek Urquhart, Mick, Michael, Peter, Colin, John D and the Eagle, John Abernethy, Patricia Marshall, Janne Møller, Alison Irvine and all at Black & White for their patience and help.

Finally, I must thank my spirit guide William and, of course, God.

Dedicated to Jessie Murphy 1950–2007 and Nina and Christopher John

CONTENTS

Introduction   1

1 A Weird and Wonderful History
   of Scottish Psychics   7

2 Spooky Weans and Dark Closes   33

3 Gallus Ghost Hunters and Graveyard   52
   Vigils

4 Face to Face with an Aberdeen Poltergeist   69

5 A Glasgow Family who Will Never Leave   89

6 Ghosts of Leisure   104

7 Psychic Animals, Ghostly Battles and   119
   Beasties

8 Goodbye and Hello Again   138

9 Getting in Tune   159

10 Forever Young   179

11 The Psychic Tourist   186

INTRODUCTION

Scotland is one of the most spiritually rich places on earth and I'm very proud to have been born here and to have experienced so many psychic and residual vibes from the many historical sites that are everywhere around us. As most of you will know, hauntings and spirits aren't limited to old castles and stately homes; there can be ghostly activity in the most unlikely of places too, including one story I heard about a spirit who seems to haunt a public lavvy!

Just imagine wherever you are at this moment in time reading this book. How many people before you have lived, breathed and died in the area around you? If you believe in the paranormal and that we are surrounded by spirit, then the chances that we will come into contact with a ghost or entity in our everyday lives and be unaware of its presence are very high indeed.

In this book I aim to share some personal psychic experiences with you. From spiritual circles in Cumbernauld to poltergeists in Aberdeen, I've been there, terrified, exhilarated, confused, overwhelmed. I never tire of learning more from the spirit world and will always try and push the boundaries of the connections I receive, either during a private sitting for someone or when I'm alone in the middle of a haunted location that seems to have a life of its own. For me, searching and communicating with elusive ghosts, phantoms – call them whatever you like – still keeps me fascinated as I seek answers to my own lifelong questions: what exactly happens after the physical body dies?

Most mediums and psychics will tell you that they know the truth about life after death and everyone else who is scientific or religious is wrong, but I personally believe that no one knows the *exact* process the essence of the human personality goes through after the flesh has ceased to be.

Through my own experiences I have come to wholeheartedly believe that the spirit does indeed go on and have received proof of that for myself and others numerous times, but when I've questioned the spirit messengers who have come through about their ethereal surroundings and everyday life around them they seem to be a bit too evasive and vague for me. For now I guess I'll have to content myself with being lucky enough to communicate with them in the first place and use the strange abilities I've developed to do some good. Who knows, maybe it's God's plan and we aren't supposed to know too much about the next stop on the path of life until we reach that destination ourselves – but I'll never give up trying to find out while I'm here.

I guess I, like many others, will always have unanswered questions that I am seeking answers for and will probably continue to investigate the paranormal and work with spirit until I'm ready to go to the other side myself. But, up until that point in my physical life, I'll have to be content with the evidence I've seen, felt and heard in my life's work as a psychic and medium, and looking back while writing this book I can see I've had some very compelling and strange experiences in my homeland that have convinced me that the afterlife is simply the next stage in the process of possible eternal life.

I decided to write this book after numerous requests by people who are fascinated by the world of psychics and who seek a deeper understanding of this life we are living and the possibility of a continuing existence in the world of spirit. To people like myself, seeing or sensing a *dead* person walking among the *living* is a part of everyday life and therefore seems perfectly normal but while writing this book I came to realise that these abilities must seem bizarre, and indeed crazy, to the interested onlooker and I completely understand why some people in this world are extremely cynical of these strange claims. All I can attempt to do within these pages is to give my honest viewpoint of personal events and experiences that have happened to me and others like me in the country of my birth and leave it up to you, the reader, to believe it or not.

Many of the people who have contacted me over the years believe they possess psychic abilities too and want to see and hear for themselves the reality of the spiritual world. With all this in mind, I have added a brief section in the book where anyone who is interested can attempt to 'tune in' to their sensitive side and even visit some of the areas I've included where I have found there to be strong energies and see what they can pick up themselves. (I'd strongly advise against sitting in the middle of a busy place meditating and calling out for spirits without permission though – you'll probably get booted out or spend a night in the police cells!)

But for anyone reading this, either psychic or not, planning a trip around this wee country and visiting varied areas that are both fascinating and beautiful will definitely cause the senses to be stirred by the immense atmosphere – and ever-changing weather – that only Scotland can bring.

This world loves labels, and people in my line of work are labelled as a 'psychic' or a 'medium' or a 'clairvoyant' or 'clairaudient' and many other titles that I'm too polite to mention! However, here in this book I'm going to try to dispense with all that and we'll concentrate more on the psychic (picking up vibes) and medium (communicating with the dead) side of my work and forget about the rest.

I'd better tell you a wee bit about myself before we continue. I was born in Kinning Park, Glasgow, in a one-bedroom, damp-ridden, tenement flat. I was brought up by my single mother and granny and am an only child who spent most of his early years lying ill with chest problems. When we moved along the Clyde to nearby Govan and I began to see and sense spirit, my whole life changed and so began the weird, secret journey of my life that has been filled with paranormal experiences.

It was only twelve years ago that I decided to come out as a psychic and medium and face the ridicule, aggression and derision from the cynics. But, whatever they say about people like me, I guess I am honoured to have been able to see the other side of life and to have been shown proof of an everlasting existence in the spirit world and of course to maybe have been able to help others along the way. I also try to be as rational as possible until I'm genuinely convinced that the phenomena myself and others are experiencing are real.

I must say I've found about ninety-nine per cent of people in spirit to be blissfully contented and happy but occasionally, at various haunted places I've visited, there lurks the darker side of spirit. In this book I'll try and show you the good and the bad side of the other world I've seen through my eyes.

I'm trying to steer clear of the usual 'psychic biography' or 'haunted handbook' type of work that fills the bookshelves, where the author only talks about himself or herself. Instead, I'll try and give you an insight into some of the strange personal experiences I've had at different locations in Scotland throughout my life, and hopefully it'll interest you.

So, dear reader, come with me to a land steeped in history – a history that is filled with love, hate, jealousy, anger and bloodshed, which can mean only one thing . . . spirits and ghosts.

Welcome to my strange world – welcome to the other side of Scotland!

1

A WEIRD AND WONDERFUL HISTORY OF SCOTTISH PSYCHICS

Some people I meet think that psychics and mediums are a relatively new phenomenon but the arts of mediumship and divination go back thousands of years in our country.

Throughout Scotland's history there has always been some fascination in psychic phenomena and after-death communication in its various forms. No doubt many of our ancestors sat around fires on cold dark evenings, telling each other stories about the souls of the dead returning to haunt the living and it's probable that the earliest tribesmen sought some form of divine guidance for their very survival against their enemies. A long time before the onslaught of present-day TV and radio psychics, there have been mediums, seers, spaewives and all manner of individuals with the gift of premonition and foresight who seem to have been an integral part of our society through the ages. This little country has had more than its fair share of ghosts, hauntings and spiritual activity since early times too and in turn has produced some very famous, and controversial, psychics and occultists.

Anyone who may have shown any signs of paranormal abilities in the distant past would probably have kept their abilities secret, due mainly to the fact that their lives would have been in danger. Many innocent people were known to have been executed throughout Europe during the tenth to the sixteenth centuries, after being branded witches by the authorities. Scotland's treatment of occult practitioners at that time was relatively tame compared to our overseas neighbours until a Witchcraft Act was passed, which meant that any poor practitioner would be tortured and burned, the same punishment as someone who had been convicted of heresy. Incidentally, murderers were treated more humanely than a so-called witch.

When King James VI came to the throne he seemed to have an obsession about witchcraft and the devil. During his reign some 'witches' from Berwick were put on trial and executed for allegedly whipping up a sea storm to drown the king and his new wife on their voyage back from Denmark. James seems to be so fanatical that he published a ridiculous book called *Daemonologie* in 1597 which was used as a guidebook by many future 'witch finders' who were swept along in the hysteria of the times. Many innocent souls suffered horrific deaths at the hands of these cruel people who used torture to ensure a confession from their victims. So, as you can guess, the age of public demonstrations of clairvoyance and mediumship was still a very long way away in those days.

I myself experienced a brief but extremely intense psychic occurrence which I believe possibly related to a witchcraft trial in a part of Edinburgh once used for executions. I have visited Castle Hill many times with friends and must admit I had never previously sensed any residual energy around the site, but then again the place was usually a bustling throng of tourists and shoppers at the time and I was more interested in the many fantastic pubs on the Royal Mile! The historical architecture and antiquity that surround the area instantly take you back in time and it's very easy for the imagination to run riot as you visualise the place in the distant past, even for someone of a non-spiritual nature. I strolled through the area alone at around 10 p.m. on my way to meet some friends. I can remember staring up at the moon shining down from the dark clear sky above. I decided to stop for a few minutes, sit down in a doorway and enjoy the calm summer night while I had the chance. I remember watching several groups of people walking around the streets quite far away and the occasional sound of the city's traffic faded into a distant drone. I decided to enjoy my rare moment of peace and take in the fantastic atmosphere around me so I closed my eyes for a second or two and took in a deep breath. Suddenly I heard the most horrific scream; I can remember the sound being quite faint but very clear. I opened my eyes and stared at the peaceful scene around me.

'Where could this scream have come from?' I asked myself.

I definitely didn't think it was a paranormal experience at that moment and was genuinely concerned for someone's safety. Then it happened again and I could tell at this point that it seemed to be coming from a dark-green coloured mist that was appearing about a hundred yards ahead of my gaze. I automatically walked over to the general area where the mist was forming and instantly felt an intense coldness. (Probably nothing paranormal there though – this is Scotland after all!) But I was then transported into a past life in my mind and could feel a burning sensation over my hands and feet and, even more alarmingly, my groin area. A sense of sheer terror and disbelief washed over me as the screams enveloped me. I knew this was definitely not my imagination and I was aware that the entity I was sensing was a female and was being watched by hundreds, maybe even thousands, of people as she slowly burned to death with her limbs bound – somewhere in the distant past. I also remember a feeling that I'd been strangled by someone earlier and had lost consciousness but woken to find myself in the fire – the emotions I felt were extremely intense. I can remember sensing the person's point of view as she helplessly attempted to beg for mercy and can still feel horror and anger to this day that her death was entertainment for the crowds. I began to feel the pain disappear as death released the poor individual from the intense agony. The screaming had now turned to moaning and somewhere in the ether was the sound of distant laughter, cheers and gasps of horror. It was then I knew this was an innocent young woman and I had a sense that the poor soul had only wanted help with pain during the birth of a child, or possibly twins, and now she was being executed as a witch! Why? That was the only information that came to my mind. Whatever the whole experience was that night, it really shocked me. As I stood there, eyes closed and still immersed in the moment around me I felt a nudge and I remember opening my eyes to be confronted by two cops.

'Are you all right, sir?' asked the big one with the moustache.

'Eh, aye I'm fine, officer,' I replied, wishing the ground would open up and swallow me.

'Can you explain to us why you're standing in the middle of the street with your eyes shut and making strange noises then?' asked the other policeman with a wee smirk on his face.

'You'd never believe me if I told ye,' I replied.

The big one with the moustache leaned in close to me. 'Have you had a lot to drink tonight, sir?'

'I haven't touched a drop yet, officers,' I answered.

He paused for a moment as his eyes stared directly into mine. 'I'd lay off the drink if I was you.'

After a few moments, they must have realised I wasn't some mad axe-wielding psycho and turned to walk away.

'The pavements are a wee bit safer. Were you never taught the Green Cross Code at school, son?' The big moustached officer asked, laughing.

It was then I realised I was slap bang in the middle of a road and could've been knocked down at any moment. I coyly made my way over to the pavement once again and smiled embarrassedly at the two bemused witnesses.

'I'm sorry, officers. It won't happen again. I was . . . eh . . . daydreamin',' I answered, with my head hung low.

As they walked away laughing, I heard the guy with the moustache say to the other, 'He's from Glesga – what do you expect?'

I did search records for some years afterwards until I found someone who had been burned to death on Castle Hill for that exact reason. One poor wee soul was murdered simply because the unbearable pain she suffered during the birth of her twins forced her to seek some herbal pain–relief from an old lady who some claimed to be a witch. So it was even dangerous to associate with witches in those days.

Was it simply my imagination playing tricks? Well, thinking back, I still think it was a genuine paranormal experience I had. It felt convincingly real to me but I guess I'll never know if it was indeed the same woman I found in the records. Paranormal or psychological, whatever happened that evening still chills me to this day and I will never forget those feelings and the sound of those screams. One thing's for sure though, I haven't walked on Edinburgh's Castle Hill alone at night since.

With the advent of science and rational thinking, the superstitious practices of days of old thankfully faded away and the burning of people alleged to practise the black arts stopped in this country long ago. But a man who was born in a remote area of this land, who undoubtedly had very strong psychic abilities, is said to have been burned to death as recently as the early 1700s.

He was one of the earliest famous Scottish psychics that I'd ever been told about and he is popularly known throughout the world as the 'Brahan Seer'. He is also sometimes known as Coinneach Odhar, and was born sometime in the middle part of the seventeenth century on the Isle of Lewis. There really isn't much known about his early life but the stories that have been passed through generations about him are as dramatic and as far-fetched as any Hollywood scriptwriter could ever muster. There are a few different stories telling of how he acquired his incredible gift of prophecy and became the possessor of a stone which allegedly held the power of his fascinating abilities but one particular story was told to me as a youngster and always scared and fascinated me as I was growing up, so this is the one I'll tell here.

I was always told that Brahan Seer's mammy was tending her cattle late one night on a ridge overlooking a burial ground when she witnessed every single grave on the site open up. She continued to watch quietly in disbelief as souls of all ages rose up from their resting places and dispersed in every direction conceivable. Instead of running away screaming (as we all probably would have done) the story goes that she waited until the ghostly inhabitants came back from their journeys a while later and lay back down in their coffins. As the earth closed over once again, everything in the burial site returned to normal and the graves appeared to be undisturbed once more . . . all except for one single grave, which remained open and unoccupied.

This very brave – or crazy – wee woman then decided that she needed a better view of the strange proceedings and made her way down to the open grave. As she entered the burial site and walked to the empty hole in the ground for closer inspection, she placed her staff into the open grave because it was believed an action like that could prevent a roaming spirit from being able to enter their resting place again. How nice of her!

A little while later a young spirit woman seemingly came floating towards the grave from a northerly direction and stopped in her tracks when she saw the staff stuck into the hole. She then turned to the Seer's mammy and asked her if she would remove the offending item because she wanted back into her hole in the ground. His mammy said to the spirit girl that she would lift her staff from the grave if she would tell her what was going on and why she had returned so late. As well as being a brave or crazy wee woman it seemed his mammy was also a busybody too, I guess.

The young woman then went on to explain that she was a princess from Norway and that somehow her body had been swept ashore on the island some time before and her remains had been interred in that grave by some kind islanders. She told mammy seer that the reason she had been away a bit longer than the other spirits was due to the distance she'd had to travel to visit her homeland across the sea.

For some strange reason, possibly out of fear or gratitude, the spirit girl told the woman that she should search a lake for a small blue stone and hand it to her young son and he would then have the incredible gift of prophecy throughout his life. It seems his mammy must have got her wellies on right away and somehow found the stone for her son, because before long it is said that the Brahan Seer had many people travelling from far and wide, seeking his services.

There are other stories about how he acquired his gift but I guess no one really knows.

However he became a seer, it does seem he was very much in demand by the gentry and upper classes of the time (as most famous psychics are), who visited him for his foresight and natural wisdom. This, coupled with his seemingly dark and sarcastic wit, entertained and mystified many but ultimately led to his own horrific death. At a meeting of aristocrats it's said that he annoyed Lady Seaforth and some of her cronies and, at her orders, the Brahan Seer was finally seized and taken away to be burned to death in a tar barrel. (Am I glad it's the twenty-first century!)

Looking back, some of the Brahan Seer's prophecies could in hindsight be put down to someone with a very keen sense of observation and it must be said, many of them haven't come true at all. For instance, he foretold some catastrophes that thankfully never happened (yet). However, he did seem to predict some modern events and many other things that have come to pass with a certain degree of accuracy. Some people to this day argue that the Brahan Seer was Scotland's answer to Nostradamus and believe in his gifts of prophecy wholeheartedly. Sadly, there aren't any definite records of him around but if we remove all of the stories and folklore that surrounds his time here, I'm sure he did exist. I believe he was simply a gifted clairvoyant with a sharp wit who would have been very popular had he lived in the present age.

There have been some books written about him that detail his premonitions and prophecies and are well worth a read for anyone interested in him.

I grew up hearing strange and far-fetched stories from my family about the Brahan Seer and must admit his life still fascinates me deeply. One day, I'm going to visit the area he resided in and try to tune into any residual energy to see if I can discover the real truth for myself about the first famous psychic in Scotland.

Like most tales from days past, his life and abilities will no doubt have been exaggerated through word of mouth over the many years since he lived and his name is now a part of Scottish folklore; but one thing's for sure, he was Scotland's first 'celebrity psychic' and who knows, maybe he was indeed accurate in *all* of his prophecies and some have still to take effect? I really hope not.

It's a pity that most people who had any kind of psychic gift in the distant past ended up being brutally executed by over-zealous crackpots or angry authorities. Thank goodness for sceptics and science!

Here's a weird wee tale of my own that I have to tell you which relates a little to the next person I'm going to talk about.

It was the early '80s and I was around sixteen or seventeen years old when I met little 'Annie'. She must have been at least in her late seventies at the time but the day she spoke to me in Cumbernauld Town Centre, I sensed there was some kind of strange spiritual connection between us. In those days, I had long hair, a leather jacket and ripped jeans and she was the epitome of a normal, wee, white-haired granny but when she spoke it was as if she had strangely known me through lifetimes and I genuinely believe that somehow the world of spirit had caused our paths to cross. Within twenty minutes or so of chatting she could tell me that I was haunted by visions of the dead and how I lay terrified in my room with the light switched on all night. I was shocked at her accuracy but still wondered if she was possibly a wee bit mad. I thought I was mad too though! She told me how 'they' wanted to talk to me or talk through me so she invited me to a small weekly spirit contact group held on a Friday afternoon in her house at three o'clock, where 'tea and cakes would be served' after the proceedings. She gave me a small piece of paper with the address scribbled on it and I promised to go along. Deep down, I had no intention of going though and gave it no more thought for the rest of the week. After a few very sleepless, eventful and scary nights of paranormal activity, I woke on the Friday morning feeling tired and weary and was feeling very upset at my nightly visions. I picked up the little scrunched-up piece of paper beside the bed and decided I would go along to this meeting out of curiosity. As I nervously knocked on the door of the house, the sound of hymns being sung to the accompaniment of a completely out-of-tune piano resonated from within. After practically breaking my knuckles trying to get an answer, there was a break in the din and Annie opened the door. She smiled and said, 'I knew you'd come along, Thomas,' and invited me in.

I entered the living room to be confronted by another four old grinning pensioners sitting in a circle with hymn-sheets in their hands. I was quickly introduced and promptly parked my rear in a spare chair in the circle. Annie sat herself down at the piano in the corner and started hammering away at the keys while the assembled group began to sing hymns very loudly with various degrees of success.

I sat in shock for a moment and was then told to join in and 'invoke the spirits'. So, after a few hymns I was singing 'What a Friend We Have in Jesus' at the top of my lungs with the rest of them. By this time I couldn't have cared less how out of tune we all were. I even managed to get the group to do a quick encore.

Finally, the time arrived. Annie sat in front of us and we all held hands as she closed her eyes and went into a trance. I watched in amazement as her face changed completely. Suddenly her face had gone and there were the features of a dark-haired young man with a small moustache. I jumped back, much to the amusement of the other spectators. One of the elderly ladies present started nagging the spirit and asked him why he hadn't visited the group for a few weeks! Then, the voice that answered her through Annie was the voice of a young man. He explained that he had been busy but loved her dearly. He then said he was waiting for her,

17

smiled and evaporated, leaving the medium's face visible again. The recipient of his message was overjoyed and it was explained to me by the man to my right that the young guy was in fact her husband who had died in World War II. After a few minutes to let Annie rest, we then closed our eyes and said prayers for our loved ones in spirit and it was during this part of the meeting that something bizarre happened to me – I am sure I somehow lifted off the chair! I thought it was my imagination and opened my eyes – but at the very moment I panicked, my butt landed back on the chair with an almighty thump. Afterwards I told Annie about my 'levitation' and she just laughed and said it had happened to some of them before – and it was usually men! I couldn't help but smile as the people there spoke about their loved ones in spirit who they chatted to weekly through Annie. I was then told that the group had been meeting like this for twenty years or so and some of the members who had passed over came to visit through Annie too.

They all agreed that I had a 'gift' and, with some development, could take over from Annie as the main spirit channel, due to her failing health.

I left her house that day enlightened yet still mystified, both at my own experience and at the transfiguration I had witnessed. I promised the group I would be back the following week but I'm really sad to say I never did return.

I passed by the wee flat a year or two later and it lay empty, so I never did get the chance to visit the group and I never saw them again.

Even now, so many years later, that strange afternoon still comes to my mind regularly – I wonder how they're all doing now in the realms of spirit. One thing's for sure though, they left this world with absolutely no doubts about their final destination and after the one day I was lucky enough to spend with those wonderful strangers, I don't have any doubts either.

I've met many psychics and mediums throughout my life and I have to say that there have been very few that I've been completely convinced by but one man I would love to have met died way back in 1886, a wee while before I was born.

This Scottish psychic medium was a very controversial figure during the Victorian era and was definitely the consummate showman. He was born in Edinburgh on 20 March 1833 and his name was Daniel Dunglas Home. For those readers who don't know much about him, there have been many biographies written that go into far more detail about his life than I can here – but let me tell you a little bit about this remarkable man and the impact he had on society in the nineteenth century.

Daniel lived with his aunt in Portobello, Scotland, for the first part of his life while his parents moved away to America to make a better life. It is said that he was a very poorly child who spent a lot of time in bed with various illnesses. He was said also to be a very nervous wee boy who seemed overly sensitive. (I personally find this seems to be the normal temperament of most people with strong psychic or mediumistic abilities.) When he finally joined his family in the USA, his aunt began to relay all the strange experiences and events that had surrounded the child while in her care and explain why she had invited three different clergymen into her house to rid the place of all the poltergeist activity surrounding the boy – all were completely unsuccessful of course, hence Daniel's return to his parents. It is said that his mother actually accepted his gift quite easily because she herself had some psychic abilities. No doubt, tales from his aunt informing her how, as a four-year-old, Daniel was able to predict future events and seemingly attract strange noises and phenomena wherever he went, probably interested her at first. But she definitely wasn't prepared for some of the crazy activity that was to follow her son around. In his autobiography *Incidents of My Life* he tells the story of how, at age thirteen, he saw his young friend who had died a while earlier visit him from beyond the grave. This seems to be his first direct communication from a spiritual entity.

As time went on, Daniel was surrounded by phenomena that definitely defied rational explanation. For instance, it is said that one time an empty chair chased his terrified sister around a room and as Daniel sat quietly smirking at the proceedings, his parents decided that he must be some kind of evil force and promptly booted him out of their house. Once again the young Daniel was away from his family and spent the next while wandering rather aimlessly, no doubt wondering what he could do with his strange gift.

His abilities and his showmanship seemed to blossom and his name soon became well known, due to his famous *physical* séances. It has to be said that Daniel never actually charged a single penny for his services. However, some of the hosts who he performed for were very wealthy individuals and were extremely hospitable towards the young man by showering him with gifts and, more importantly, giving him somewhere to lay his head down at night.

His astounding feats of physical mediumship, which included regularly levitating in the air and making his body seemingly grow an extra foot in length, both horrified and fascinated onlookers, and the unnerving accuracy of his readings to various sitters also caused some shock.

He later returned to Britain, where he succeeded in convincing many sceptical onlookers that his otherworldly demonstrations were genuine and not merely magic parlour tricks that most other Victorian mediums were resorting to. It must be said that Daniel's séances were usually performed in well-lit rooms, sometimes under rather strict conditions, so the chances of fraud were slim. By this time, spiritual hands were allegedly manifesting and evaporating in front of people's eyes and his name and reputation were becoming well known in aristocratic circles.

In 1859 Daniel met Mlle Alexandrina de Kroll and they married in St Petersburg. Together they had a young son but sadly his wife died after only four years of marriage. This left him as a single parent and it is documented that he lectured on spiritualism for a while before unsuccessfully attempting to become a sculptor. This was only a short-lived escape from his work as a medium as before long he was performing in parlour rooms once again. It was around this time that Daniel performed the most amazing feat of his career. At a house of a Mr Hall, Daniel seemingly levitated and floated out of a third-storey window and returned to the room the same way. This was done in a room filled with onlookers who were completely in shock at this impossible feat.

But no matter how many people he convinced privately, he had many detractors who despised him and would never believe in him. He had insulting poems and distorted articles written about him in the press, as well as the usual attacks that psychics receive from magicians.

Even though he was still a relatively young guy, his health was deteriorating and it is said that his séances became very poor compared with those of earlier times. Sir William Crookes, an eminent scientist at the time, seemed highly impressed with Daniel's abilities and wrote that he could find no evidence of trickery or deception with him. However, some of the absurd information Daniel's spirit control would spout was complete nonsense. For instance, his control once told some assembled guests that the sun was actually cold! But then again, who says all spirit guides and controls have to be intelligent? (NB: A 'spirit control' is an entity who helps the medium achieve contact with the spirit world. It is sometimes also referred to as a 'spirit guide'.)

That afternoon over twenty years ago when I witnessed the most incredible transfiguration and felt myself begin to lift off the chair still makes me question my state of mind that day. Was it spiritual? Or was I simply carried away with the bizarre proceedings? (For any spirit to lift me, they would have to be *very* strong, believe me!) I genuinely sensed myself rising up higher and higher that day and am ninety-nine per cent sure I was elevated a few inches off the floor for a few moments. I am very aware of the workings of the mind during relaxation and know that sometimes a person can feel these sensations during an altered brain state but this seemed different. This has caused me to re-evaluate my thoughts and has opened my mind to the possibility that some of Daniel's physical feats could have been genuine. Before my own experience, I was convinced that all shows of levitation were fraudulent and done only by the methods magicians use – for instance the 'Balducci levitation' (a trick where the performer stands up on one toe and it seems he is levitating from an angle) as performed by numerous street illusionists nowadays – but now I'm not so sure. Maybe it was imagination? I've never been able to achieve that feeling again but here's hoping – I'll just have to make sure everyone's well out of the way when I fall back to earth again! Anyway, back to Daniel . . .

He then married a rich Russian woman called Julie de Gloumeline and became rather reclusive, ending his days in the Mediterranean where the weather helped ease his health problems relating to his chest.

As I stated earlier, he died in 1886. He was laid to rest in Paris. Many books have been written about the life of Daniel Dunglas Home and, even now, so many years later, his feats are still controversial and opinion is divided. Was he the real deal? In my personal opinion I think he was a great medium who possibly used some trickery to gain fame and attention but I guess every reader will come to their own conclusions.

In the Canongate in Edinburgh, a fountain was erected to his memory opposite the Canongate Parish Church; a fitting reminder of the greatest physical medium of all time . . . or should that be the greatest *magician*? We will never know.

Before I continue on this short whirlwind tour of some Scottish psychic history, I'll tell you a wee story about a strange event I was invited to when I was about seventeen years old. The relevance of the experience will become apparent later on.

Throughout my early life and psychic experiences, I kept my contact with the spirit world a secret. I was scared of being laughed at and decided to tell absolutely no one in case they thought I was crazy. After all, not one person I knew growing up around me at that time saw spirit people and had long conversations with the dead like I did. I felt ashamed of my secret life and vowed never to tell a living soul but the stress of keeping it all to myself sometimes deeply disturbed me. One evening this was all to change when I was introduced to a girl at an Ozzy Osbourne gig and after a while she told me she went to private meetings with the best medium, healer and psychic ever. I quietly screamed with happiness but kept my cool on the outside, of course. I told her I would like to visit this person but, deep down, I really wanted someone to help explain why I was cursed with this spiritual nightmare and tell me why the spirits had picked on me.

I met the girl the following Thursday evening at Boots' Corner in Glasgow and took the subway with her over to Byres Road, in the west end of the city. I remember climbing to the top floor of a tenement flat just off the aforementioned street. I was very surprised to see the girl had two boxes of Tunnock's tea cakes and some Empire biscuits in a bag with her but didn't give it too much thought at the time. When we breathlessly reached our destination she knocked on a door and a few moments later it was answered by a wee old woman wearing a blouse covered in suspicious-looking brown stains. She took a moment to eye me up and down suspiciously then gestured for us to enter. The smell of whisky from her breath nearly knocked me out as she grabbed the bag of tea cakes and biscuits from the girl's hand then escorted us into the lounge area and said to both of us, 'That'll be forty-five each darlings.' I forced a smile as I grudgingly placed the £90 in her hands and told the girl to put her money back in her pocket. I imagined that this meeting with a genuine mystic and healer would probably be worth every penny and, although I wouldn't eat for a week, I decided that it was worth paying the girl's fee simply for introducing me to this person. I sat back on the settee nervously in anticipation of my meeting. The wee woman promptly shoved the money down her stained blouse and said, 'She'll be a hauf an hour, OK. And nae cameras or recorders or ye're oot on yer arses . . . God bless ye darlings.' There was another knock on the door and two elderly women were ushered in and seated across from us. They spent the next ten minutes or so trying to hide their disdain at the long haired, leather-clad lump that sat in front of them, i.e. yours truly!

The wee old woman who was in charge of the proceedings came staggering back in with a huge plate piled high with the tea cakes and Empire biscuits and placed it on the table – well out of our reach of course. She then promptly took the other women's money with equal vigour and again stuffed it down her blouse and informed them that the proceedings would start in 'hauf an hour'. She drew me a warning glance when she noticed my eyes staring longingly at the pile of tea cakes at the far end of the room.

'That's sugar for the spirit world. The medium needs lotsa sugar,' she informed me with a threatening snarl.

She then hurried across to the window and drew the curtains. Some candles that were on the table were ceremoniously lit and the scene was now set for the star of the proceedings to take centre stage.

In walked a huge woman in her fifties who had her hair dyed the blackest colour imaginable, huge gold earrings, a loose-fitting black kaftan and make-up that looked as if it had been applied with a shovel. She sat down on a creaky chair and paused for a moment. We all sat in awe awaiting her words . . . 'Hey, Maisie, the spirits need sugar.' At this, the old woman poured her a huge glass of Irn-Bru and handed her a tea cake – both were guzzled down within seconds.

She then sat back, closed here eyes and said, 'Who's Tam?'

'That's . . . eh . . . me, I think,' I stuttered nervously.

One of her eyes opened and peeped curiously in my direction as I excitedly awaited some message of hope and deep meaning . . .

'Your granny says you should get your hair cut.' She then closed her eye again and continued. 'Is there a . . . Mary here?' she asked.

One of the wee women began to tremble with either fear or excitement . . . 'Oh, that's me, dear,' she replied.

'Your man's here, Mary. He says do you remember the wee budgie?'

The wee woman was now jumping for joy. 'Oh, I do. Are they together?' she asked.

The mystic paused. 'It's sitting on your man's hand in heaven. He's saying "God bless you", sweetie.'

The wee woman looked delighted. 'Oh that's just wonderful! I tried for years to get him to talk but he would just sit there and whistle,' she informed everyone as she dabbed her eyes.

I had to stop myself doubling up with laughter as our mystic looked puzzled and ever so slightly annoyed.

'It was your husband that said "God bless you", Mary, not the bloody budgie!' she yelled.

The wee woman looked so disappointed!

After some vague stabs at information towards the other two sitters, I felt my heart begin to sink as I knew my £90 had been well and truly wasted. But the best was still to come. Wee 'Maisie' was told to tie the mystic's hands to her chair and we were then informed by Maisie that there may or may not be a manifestation of ectoplasm from the spirit world through the medium.

The lights were dimmed by extinguishing candles in the room and after a few moments in near pitch black, our star began to make gurgling and retching noises and before long, a thin white mass began to ooze from her mouth slowly down her body. In the near pitch-black room it was very difficult to make out much but I sat in horror as the smell of vomit mixed with extinguished candle smoke and Maisie's whisky-breath filled the room. Gasps of amazement came from the other three sitters but, to me, the 'ectoplasm' looked suspiciously like wet regurgitated cloth of some sort. I could even see it had square edges! I genuinely felt like storming out but sat there and suffered the proceedings – and the smell – for the next five minutes or so as the medium swallowed the cloth . . . or should I say ectoplasm down again.

She was then untied and led from the room by her drunken, elderly assistant and we were all left sitting in the dark twiddling our thumbs. Then Maisie came back in, opened the curtains and with a loud 'God bless ye all darlings' she pointed to the door for us to go.

We were all then led out by our four-foot-eight, silver-haired, drunk Gestapo chief – who now had a few extra stains on her blouse and 180 quid poking out from her cleavage. We all descended the stairs to a shout of

'Remember and shut the door of the close behind ye . . . God bless ye darlings!' ringing in our ears from a very drunk Maisie from the landing above.

I made my excuses afterwards and went home penniless and disappointed. I never did see the girl again and must admit, was devastated that people would actually resort to such nonsense.

I've never witnessed anyone attempting to produce ectoplasm again and still remain sceptical, but I hope one day I'm proved wrong. This all leads me on to a notorious case of a wee woman who allegedly produced ectoplasm and full-figure manifestations during her séances and ended up paying the price for her gift of mediumship by being tried with conspiracy, vagrancy and witchcraft and tragically sent to prison. For any readers unaware of the case, this didn't happen hundreds of years ago – this was during World War II.

Helen Duncan was born in Callander on 25 November 1897 and rose to become a very well-respected medium and channel for the departed. It is said that full-body materialisations of dead relatives would appear at her meetings and they would convey information that was unnervingly accurate to the sitters, while Helen would sit in a trance state.

During the time of war, anxious relatives of servicemen and women would visit Helen and it is said her abilities were undoubted by most involved. But one such session would cost Mrs Duncan her reputation, her freedom and, some say, ultimately her life.

It was in the town of Portsmouth that her world came crashing down when a spirit sailor informed an audience that a warship, HMS *Barham*, had sunk – this was before the details of any sinking had been released to the public. It wasn't long before she was taken by the police and tried under the ridiculous Witchcraft Act and sentenced to nine months imprisonment. It is said that all of this hysteria was caused by the fear that the date of the Normandy D-Day landings would be revealed by her but this was never officially given as a reason.

Afterwards, Helen's life was never the same and it seems she was hounded by the authorities and her séances were raided, even after the war had ended. In 1956, the police – obviously for want of something better to do – raided one of her meetings to prove she was fraudulent. Afterwards a doctor discovered two second degree burns on her stomach and released her. She then came back home to Scotland, was admitted to hospital and sadly died soon afterwards.

When I look at photographs of Helen Duncan allegedly producing ectoplasm it all looks so false and indeed ridiculous, but it can't be underestimated that she helped many people through one of the worst times in recent history with accurate messages of comfort which I'm sure were from the other side of life. At the time of writing, all these years later, many people still want her to be pardoned.

Some people will say that once a fraud, always a fraud, but most if not all of her clients have since passed away and I'm sure that most of them would beg to differ with that opinion. Whatever we think about the wee housewife and mother from a small Scottish town who suffered a major miscarriage of justice at the hands of a paranoid government, she will forever be remembered as the last official witch in Scotland.

It would be nigh on impossible to list in this book every psychic practitioner and researcher this country has produced over the years, but I'd like to thank them all for withstanding the scorn, insults and ridicule some cynics have shown towards them throughout history. If it wasn't for the research work of people like Arthur Findlay, the founder of the Glasgow Society for Psychical Research, or the charitable openness of the Glasgow physical medium, John Sloan, who never charged a single penny in his life for his demonstrations and left himself open to scientific scrutiny, then all psychics and mediums may still be treated as criminals today.

Even now, many sceptics think of believers in the paranormal as crazy people but a recent survey claimed that more than half of people in the United Kingdom believe in psychic abilities. They can't all be wrong, surely? Every person's experience of life is subjective and my own experiences will obviously differ greatly from someone who is scientifically minded. I believe I am very rationally minded and will only stand by a belief if it has been proved to me beyond doubt. That's why I refuse to believe in fairies, goblins, ectoplasm, auras etc. until I see them with my own eyes. I will never scorn others who do claim to have had those experiences though. After all, who am I to laugh? I have seen the dead and I have heard the dead and I have received information from numerous sitters through means that delve far deeper than cold reading. So, I believe anything is possible.

Sadly, fraudsters invade all aspects of life and the spiritualist world has had more than its fair share of con artists and crooks throughout history and Scotland is no exception. It's true that some troubled or grieving individuals, desperate to hear a message from a loved one or hoping to be told something great for the future, will often pay a lot of money and accept vague information from dodgy psychics and fill in the gaps themselves. However, I find most people who visit mediums or attend meetings are sane, rational human beings who are simply happy to know that life does go on after the breakdown of the physical body and that our friends and family members are just a step ahead of us.

Some prominent key figures in recent history have supported spiritualism and a belief in the afterlife. The Edinburgh writer, Arthur Conan Doyle, who penned the Sherlock Holmes books, was a convinced spiritualist and argued the case for life after death but lost credibility with some peers for his deep belief in the Cottingley Fairies, a series of photographs by two young girls allegedly showing themselves posing with fairies. (The girls later admitted that they took the photos fraudulently.) Arthur failed to convince some friends and acquaintances that his views were valid but he remained convinced throughout his physical life.

As I said earlier in this chapter, this book is by no means an exhaustive list of Scottish psychics, mediums, hauntings or ghosts. There are many history books on the shelves that go into far greater detail than can I talk about here about the personalities involved in the movement, but I hope you can see that this rainy, wee country has produced some excellent and colourful characters that have served the world of spirit – and still do. What follows now are some investigations and experiences I've known about or been involved in throughout my life . . . it's up to you to decide for yourself whether the experiences were real or simply an overactive imagination at work and the author just talking mince! All I can say is that every psychic or spiritual encounter that follows was very real, and occasionally scary, to me and any others involved . . .

2

SPOOKY WEANS AND DARK CLOSES

Most of you will have noticed that in recent times there has been a huge rise in paranormal TV shows, radio shows, New-Age magazines and, ahem . . . books by psychics! It seems that ghosts, spirits and life after death have never been as popular as they are now. This media coverage has spawned a huge rise in the number of haunted investigation groups springing up throughout the UK and indeed the rest of the world. The usual set-up (but not always) for these groups consists of some of the members using scientific and traditional ghost-hunting equipment – which I'll tell you about later in this book – and someone in the group who is of a sensitive nature, who can maybe pick up on vibrations that others can't. In other words, this person will be a psychic or medium, who will join the investigation (or invest) with the group and try to receive contact or attempt to tune in to the residual energy that may still be active in the location. All the group needs then is an alleged haunted location, nerves of steel and a few hours to investigate. In a moment I'll tell you about some personal scary experiences and investigations I've been involved in over the years – I have to admit some of it still causes me nightmares occasionally, but for now let me talk a wee bit more about 'ghost hunting' .

There are many books on the shelves detailing famous haunted locations and most are filled with tales of the ghosts of long-dead kings and queens who, it's said, still seem to be floating through the dark corridors of lavish stately homes and castles long after their physical demise. For instance, Mary Queen of Scots must be a very busy lady in the afterlife. I've been told she can be seen in at least five different locations throughout the whole of the UK. If some guide books were to be believed, our wee Mary hasn't got a minute to herself as she allegedly floats around (it seems wearing her head or not is optional) at locations that are hundreds of miles apart – and sometimes she's seen in two places at the same time.

There have been many documented sightings of grey ladies, white ladies, blue ladies and green ladies witnessed in many of Scotland's historic buildings and landscapes, and although this kind of apparition does interest me, I always attempt to delve deeper into any spiritual contact. The sight of some genuine poltergeist activity or definite communication are the only phenomena that really impress me.

I have to say that any time I've attended a paranormal investigation of a historic building or landmark I've rarely witnessed any activity that's startled me and I'm sad to say I've never sensed anyone famous – or infamous either.

We must remember that the human mind can play tricks in a shadowy, draughty, old baronial house in the dead of night and some less experienced paranormal investigators or psychics can let their imaginations run riot! (Mine used to.) I believe we should always remain sceptical until we know for a fact that our eyes, ears or minds aren't deceiving us and only then can we separate reality from fiction. During these types of vigils in these types of locations I tend to try to pick up on the residual energy there or communicate with the active spirits of butlers, maids, cooks and guards etc. who also resided within the walls of these locations and have their own stories to tell. And if a king or a queen 'pops in' to say hello I'll gladly act as medium for them – but they very rarely do.

The current trend for paranormal programming has brought the world of psychics and spiritualist mediums much publicity, both positive and negative, mainly due to the larger than life characters who star in these shows. Many people who come to see me for the first time having only seen mediums on the telly ask if I'll be *possessed* by someone and run around the room growling and screaming during the reading. I always reply that I hope not and if I do, please phone me a doctor!

On a few rare occasions I have allowed spirit entities present to talk through me at investigations but I have to say I really don't like the thought of someone else – either alive or dead – being in control of me, and once or twice in the past, a negative force has made itself present and the situation has became dangerous for all involved, so I try to avoid a 'takeover'.

Thankfully, the everyday spiritual communication I receive is completely different from these experiences and a message from spirit is usually given through the love of someone on the 'other side' attempting to tell their grieving loved ones in this side of life that they are happy and well. The small details that spirit gives – for instance, certain dates, names or even some mundane information known only to the loved one – are merely a formality and are really only to validate their existence. From spirit's point of view, all the medium would really need to say on their behalf during a floorshow or a private sitting is

'We're happy and we love you' but no one in this world would believe the medium and would still need some definite confirmation and proof that it was indeed their loved one communicating – and quite rightly so.

However, as I've already mentioned, I've also seen the more evil side of the spirit world throughout my work and will categorically say that some deceased individuals can, on occasion, be a lot more scary than the living.

What follows are a few experiences with the darker side of spirit and some investigations, both personal and professional, that have basically given me the willies.

I've personally found that some of the most *active* haunted locations I've witnessed aren't deeply historic places or old dwellings. Some of the most frightening events I've been lucky (or unlucky) enough to have been present at have been in private houses in housing schemes, desolate farms, leafy west end tenements or suburban houses. I'm contacted regularly by many families who seek absolutely no publicity and are usually ashamed to let it be known publicly that they believe they are being terrorised by ghostly inhabitants in their own homes. But when all other avenues have been explored and they are at their wits end they contact someone like yours truly.

I understand completely the feelings of hopelessness and loneliness that some of these poor people have to endure as their lives are ruined by unknown visitors causing disturbances and creating havoc. And the worst part of this very real problem? – some people don't believe such things even exist.

I've been involved in loads of these private paranormal investigations throughout my life (which I've never charged a fee for) and they usually take place in the least likely of locations; old or modern homes and flats, some of which I'll tell you about later in this book.

I must admit I've always had a real mission to come to the aid of people who are being disturbed by hauntings in their own homes. I always try to dedicate as much time as I can to ease their suffering by attempting to help any spirit 'move on' or by finding rational explanations to phenomena. Why? Well, I think it could be because my entire childhood was ruined by manifestations and ghosts in the homes we lived in and I know how stressful it can be.

Occasionally, some personal psychic experiences that have happened to me in my early years still nag away at me even to this day and I get this strange and intense urge to revisit the paranormal places from my past and attempt to find out exactly what really happened to that wee boy who lay terrified at the visions around him. Well, I recently did just that with one particular place I used to live in. Before I tell you about the day I returned, I'll tell you why I felt so compelled to go back in the first place.

It all happened when I was a wee boy, about four years old, living in an old tenement flat on Langlands Road in Govan, Glasgow.

I became friends with a young spirit boy called 'Andrew' who would visit me regularly – he was completely solid to me and definitely didn't look like a spirit. It wasn't until many months later that he informed me that he was actually dead! I loved the time I spent with him in that wee house and genuinely didn't imagine he was anything other than alive. I even introduced him to my mother and granny who spoke to him too – I think they may have been patronising me! (Many years later my granny swore to me that she did see him once or twice though.) After a while, Andrew's visits became few and far between and practically ceased for a while. It was during this time that something a little more sinister happened to me which was the cause of many years of analysing.

I was alone playing on the bed in the kitchen one day. (This may sound strange to some young or posh readers but there was a recess in the wall of the kitchen and that's where my mother and I slept. My granny slept on the settee in the room next door.) Suddenly, there was the distinct sound of children playing in our wee hall.

'Ring a ring a roses, a pocketful of posies . . . '

I quickly dropped my toys and ran out excitedly, thinking Andrew had returned. But there was nothing. I was standing there all alone in the silent lobby. I remember walking dejectedly back into the kitchen and lying on the bed. I sobbed my heart out. My only real friend had gone and there seemed no sign of his return. Then the faint sound of 'ring a ring a roses' emanated from the hall again . . . I looked again but still there was nothing.

About a week later, on a Saturday afternoon, I was sitting with my granny watching the wrestling on the old telly we had been given. The vertical hold on the thing had gone so we watched programmes with a constant vertical line moving up and down the screen. Amazing how you get used to that after a while! My wee granny used to get extremely excited when the wrestling was on and was known to shout at the box. The patter was hilarious and it was known for neighbours to visit during that time to witness her enthusiasm and rage. All I can say is, if that wee four-foot-eleven grey-haired woman had got a hold of wrestling 'baddies' Mick McManus or Steve Logan, they'd have been in serious trouble! I loved it.

That afternoon though, my mother was out and it was just the two of us alone in the house. Through the combined din of the telly and my granny's yelling I heard voices in the hall again singing 'ring a ring a roses'. I turned and, through the smoked glass of the door (it was the 1970s, remember), I was sure I saw a dark figure move past the other side of the door.

I ran out as fast as I could but again there was no one there. This time, an unbelievably strong, icy chill was in the air and a strange smell of freshly-dug earth. I knew there was *something* there.

'Hello?' I whispered quietly towards the dark corners.

From the living room I could still hear my granny's voice shouting encouragement to the wrestlers as if she was in their corner – 'Grab him by the ears!' I stared around at the dark wee hall and attempted contact again.

'Andrew? Is that you?' I asked, hoping to encourage a response.

Another shout echoed from the room. 'Break it! Break it . . . Grab his nose!'

My granny was clearly having the time of her life as she saw the villain of the ring get his comeuppance – tea and fag ash were flying everywhere as she jumped about her chair in excitement.

As I listened again I was suddenly tapped on the head from behind. I turned and saw a fleeting dark shadow dart by. I was then tapped on my shoulder from behind again. A chill went down my back as I quickly turned again, only to see the speeding black figure disappear. A mix of excitement and a little trepidation filled my every sense. Goosebumps rose on my arms.

'Want tae play?' I asked.

Suddenly I felt my trousers being pulled! Then I heard laughter coming from the kitchen area as a fleeting shadow ran through the door. I ran in after the figure and so began a game of hide and seek throughout that wee flat that lasted quite a while if I remember correctly. I finally looked in the old wardrobe that stood in the hall and nearly fainted as they both jumped out – a boy and a girl who were dressed in what I can only describe as dark-coloured rags. Thinking back, I remember that their clothes looked very coarse and their skin had a faint blue tinge. I've never seen spirit looking like that since I must say.

The wee girl had a pretty face and very long dark hair and the boy had very short dark hair and both had eyes that seemed black in colour. Sounds like something from a horror movie I suppose but their faces are as clear as could be in my mind even to this day. No wonder I was feart!

The boy was the elder of the two, I think. I also distinctly remember they were both in their bare feet which amused me. The three of us stood there in silence as they sneered, while the distant shouts of my granny continued.

'Who are ye?' I enquired.

They mischievously grinned at each other then both turned and stared directly into my eyes.

I asked again, 'What are yer names? I'm Thomas. Do ye know Andrew?'

They looked at each other again and began to dance in a circle around me, silently laughing.

I couldn't hear a sound from them but their evil, grinning faces going round in circles began to really scare me. I knew for a fact they were *dead*!

'Gonnae stop it, please?' I begged.

But still they continued to dance round me, faster and faster . . . grinning and dancing.

'Stop it,' I screamed but they continued round and round, causing me to feel sick and dizzy.

Suddenly I staggered through the boy and ran into the room where my granny was. I was chilled to the bone and obviously looking off colour.

'Ye OK, son?' she asked. 'You're awful peely-wally.'

'Aye, Granny, I'm OK,' I answered nervously. I could still hear giggling coming from the hall.

'Do ye need tae go down the stair tae the toilet, son?' Granny asked.

'Aye, Granny, I need a pee,' I replied as she led me out the door and past the two children who now stared solemnly at both of us.

I just couldn't wait to get out of that house, even if it was only for a few minutes. The outside toilet we used was shared by a good few families and was down the stairs from us. I was never allowed to go myself and was actually quite thankful for that. All sorts of strange characters would hang around our close due to its proximity with the Waverley pub next door and it was definitely out of bounds for a wee boy. I entered the dank dark toilet which I remember always seemed to be freezing cold. Instead of toilet paper the neighbours had cut out perfect wee squares of newspaper and hung them up. I can always say I walked about with yesterday's news stories printed on my bum! At that moment I only had one thing on my mind though – who were these new scary visitors?

As we climbed the stairs back up to our flat, they stood at our landing above and grinned down at us. I can remember being surprised that my granny didn't seem to notice them but she did remark on how icy-cold the house had become as we walked back in our door. Strangely, the telly had been switched off. I later found out that my mother and granny knew for a fact the house was haunted but didn't want to frighten yours truly. Some chance!

After that first appearance, they used to appear regularly at night for a while and play about the hall – even my mother saw them and screamed one time as she noticed them peering through the glass door at her.

A few weeks passed and the memory and fear of their visits gradually faded as life went back to normal.

There were no children living up our close and I had extremely bad chest problems so I spent most of my time stuck in the house. Noticing my sadness and loneliness, my mother brought a wee mongrel puppy for me called Honey. She was a great wee dog and a real companion for me. She followed me about the house and we would play for hours but she would never stay in the hall herself and used to growl at the wardrobe all the time. One day I was in the kitchen again playing with Honey and heard a knocking sound coming from beneath the sink.

Honey began to growl at the area as the hairs on her back rose up. I slowly walked over, thinking it couldn't be anything other than a mouse or a rat. Our building had been infested with mice and the occasional rat since we moved in. By this time too, the water in the building had been turned off because some burst pipe in the back had been flooding the place for months. To get any water we all had to go down to the street with a big key and turn it on, run upstairs, fill up pots and run back down again to turn it off. So, I was used to strange noises coming from the pipes. This time though the rapping sound was different. It was loud and definitely coming from behind the door of the cupboard. I walked over and opened the wee door and before I could even say anything, the boy and girl appeared behind me, grabbed me by the shirt and tried to throw me out of the window. All I could hear was one of them saying something about 'playing with them forever'.

Honey began to go crazy, barking and attempting to bite them but obviously to no avail. Even though we were only one storey up, it was a hell of a long way down for a four-year-old. I fought with them for what seemed like ten minutes until my granny and mother came running in and they disappeared. I have since been told the situation only lasted about half a minute or so – it definitely seemed a lot longer than that for me though.

That night in bed as everyone was asleep I lay awake in fear. My mother kept a night light on because of my fear of the visitors. As I lay cuddling into my mother while Honey lay at my feet faithfully, I began to relax and slowly drift off. I was quickly woken up by a vision of the little girl floating around the room. She looked very serious and was pointing at Honey, who had by this time woken up and had started growling at the apparition.

'He's gonnae do somethin' bad to the dog. He's angry,' I heard from her in my mind.

She then reached out and touched my face, and it felt like an icy feather – if you can imagine such a bizarre thing. I have to admit I was completely frozen with fear and unable even to utter a word in response.

'Have ye seen my mammy?' she asked softly as Honey began to advance towards her.

The girl then faded and pointed to Honey once again as she stared at my wee dog with a sad expression on her face.

The atmosphere instantly lightened as she evaporated into a mist and then into the darkness. Honey jumped back up beside me and laid her wee head on my arm. I cuddled her and knew that with this little furry companion by my side I wouldn't be alone. I then woke my mother up and told her I was scared again. She held me close and I quickly drifted off to sleep for the night. I felt safe, warm and secure and thankfully I never heard from or saw the two spirits again. Sadly, I was soon scared, alone and heartbroken once more because my wee dog Honey collapsed and died two days later.

I only saw Andrew one more time, a week or so before we were to move away. I vividly remember him standing silently in the hall. He looked into my eyes, smiled and vanished and I didn't get the chance to talk to him again until the day we were moving to a new house. I remember looking up from the removal van at the dirty old building and those bare windows above and seeing him staring forlornly out, seemingly into space. Behind him was the outline of an elderly woman. As the van pulled away taking us to a new life somewhere else, I cried and waved up at his figure but he didn't react at all. In fact, he didn't even look at me once. The building was demolished a year later.

That episode of my life has always puzzled and at times disturbed me. Although I've passed through the area a few times over the years for different reasons, my mind always travels back to those days. I've never really attempted to pick up residual vibes or attempted to find out if those scary visits were figments of imagination from a lonely wee boy or indeed were my first contact with the afterlife. I always intended to try and find out and recently I revisited the scene in an attempt to possibly gain some closure.

So, forward to 2007. In February, on the way to another private ghost hunt, I decided to stop off in Govan again for a bit of nostalgia and attempted to locate the spot where the close I lived in once stood. Most tenements in Glasgow were wiped away by the city developers in the name of progress and Langlands Road was no exception. The place has changed beyond all recognition today and it really is difficult to get a sense of perspective. The tall, grey foreboding buildings that once lined each side of the long street, blocking out the daylight above, have been replaced by a mixture of smaller, modern houses that have improved the place beyond belief.

However, along with my old mate, veteran ghost hunter, Tom M, I attempted to find out if any residual energy still exists there. Tom M used the EMF meter (see page 52 for details) when I approached the area and the needle went haywire as I attempted to contact the childhood spirits. Tom M, being a sceptic, said there were probably too many non-paranormal reasons why this would happen, and it was probably due to the fact that we were standing directly in the middle of a street. As I 'tuned in', I have to say I was very sad to find absolutely no sign or trace of Andrew. I definitely sensed two other children though, a boy and a girl, but didn't get enough information (i.e. names etc.) to find out for certain if they were the same young visitors who terrorised me as a wee boy. I did see a disturbing mental image, however, of two small bodies drowning in the dark waters of the nearby River Clyde while a drunken man lay on the riverbank laughing. But was this my subconscious memories 'creating a story' or genuine psychic information? I'm quite sure it was psychic information but I guess many sceptics, like Tom M, would disagree with me and prefer that I walk in 'cold' (i.e. with no prior knowledge or information) to a location. Then again, this visit wasn't an *official* investigation and was uniquely personal to me but I still approached it all as objectively as I could.

Standing around Hills Trust, my first school, again I could feel nothing except for the normal feelings of nostalgia and faded memories you get as time goes by. So we continued to walk around Govan, and I have to admit I was feeling rather disappointed and frustrated at not sensing any definite trace of the spirits of the past. On we continued in hope . . .

Something very strange happened though as we walked along to Govan Cross, that was to take me by surprise. As we passed 'The Black Man', a statue at the cross, I saw an old man standing outside Brechin's pub. He was wearing a cloth cap and looked absolutely filthy – then quick as a flash, he disappeared in front of my eyes. I was over the moon! Ghosts were out in Govan!

I then asked Tom M to walk along Govan Road with me because of my fascination with a story I was told many years ago by my granny. It was about an elderly lady who hung out of her window every night and smiled down at my uncle and his workmates when they were working nights in the area, in the late '50s. It was only when he walked past the house one day that he noticed the house was empty and he later found out she had taken her own life some months before. There are relatively few details known about her and it has always interested me since. As we walked along the pavement that cold evening, I sensed several spirits and one area of the road in particular seemed to resonate with the dark residual energy of some brutal murder. I'm sad to report I didn't sense anything from the old woman who it is said left this life in such a strange and disturbing way on that street fifty years ago.

We then decided to visit Govan Old Parish Church Graveyard.

Now, this place is a psychic's dream! Imagine if you will, Sauchiehall Street in Glasgow, or Edinburgh's Princes Street on a Saturday afternoon. Imagine all those strangers walking by you – some are silent and some are talking to friends who are walking beside them. To your ears, the overall sound becomes inaudible, except for the occasional snippets of conversation that you pick up. Well, places as *active* as Govan Old Parish Church Graveyard are the psychic and spiritual equivalent to that!

I normally find graveyards deserted of spirits, except maybe for the random ghostly visitor, but this location was so packed with the *living* dead it practically took my breath away as we entered.

When I was growing up I used to sneak away and walk around many graveyards and read the inscriptions of the stones, so my fascination runs very deep indeed.

I must say though, I had always wanted to visit this place but had always passed it by. However, that day I knew we had to go in and now am very glad we did.

Govan Old Parish Church (c.1888) has some of the oldest Christian carved stones, some even dating over 1000 years old and is itself a wonderfully spiritual and phenomenally interesting place. But the graveyard for me has some fantastic connections.

As we entered the location I saw a monk-like figure, head bowed, standing at one of the graves. Incidentally, my sceptical friend, Tom M, saw 'something strange' on the infrared thermometer he used at that spot too but refused to admit or deny it was an apparition, instead focusing on the possibility of a breeze. As I closed my eyes and concentrated, I could hear hushed voices speaking in Gaelic and sadly couldn't understand a word they were saying to each other but I knew for a fact they weren't speaking directly to me. I wasn't even sure if they were aware of our presence at that moment and it may have been residual playback. (Residual playback is said to occur when a ghostly scene is 'replayed' over and over again, like in a film. I talk about this later in the book.)

When I opened my eyes again I could see eight spiritual figures moving around the area. Two of them were definitely female. It was hard to tell their ages but I'd hazard a guess at forty to fifty years old. They were both wearing shawls, one had her hair tied back in a bun and the other seemed to have a black scarf on her head. They seemed totally unaware of us as we approached and they remained visible to me until I was maybe five or six feet away. Tom M reported strong activity on the EMF meter but, as usual, saw nothing. Four of the entities were small and seemed to be children but I couldn't get a clear enough view as they appeared shadow-like to my physical eyes. As I attempted contact they seemed shy and faded away.

After ten minutes or so of trying to decipher some voices in the 'crowd', I managed to make out a spirit voice with an English accent. I was surprised, to say the least, but he introduced himself as George and explained how he loved being there. He explained that he had died in 1779 and was a sailor but – and this is strange even to me – he wasn't sure *how* he died!

He explained that he became so drunk one night that he passed out on some common ground called 'Fairfield's Land' (we later found out that's where Elder Park is now situated) and all of a sudden he *woke up* and was in spirit. He then explained that he was originally from Manchester.

I offered him some prayers to attempt to help him 'move on' but he surprisingly seemed a bit peeved at my offer and said he was 'very happy where I am, thank you very much sir.' He whistled an unknown tune (that I can't get out of my head and is driving me crazy!) then simply smiled and walked away into a shadowy corner and vanished.

A wee while later there was another male spirit present but the connection was so faint it was hardly audible at all. I do know he was speaking in a broad Scots dialect and I'm sure he called me a 'swine' at one point. It was at this stage in the proceedings that we decided to exit the beautiful graveyard and leave Old Govan Parish Church and indeed the area of Govan behind for the night.

Well, it just goes to show that when it comes to spirit contact and the paranormal, we should always expect the unexpected. I had travelled back to the scene of my childhood home, hoping for something concrete in my mind that could possibly take away those uneasy feelings

I get whenever I think of that little spirit boy, Andrew. Sadly, the only definite *ghosts* I believe I saw on Langlands Road that day were in my own mind; faded memories of my granny, of my late mother as a young girl waiting at the school gates for her wee boy, of my wee dog Honey, of Saturday wrestling, of innocence and fear. I did, however, experience incredible psychic activity in other parts of that great wee 'fishing village' called Govan that I'm glad to have been able to relate to you here. The graveyard was an amazing psychic experience and I'm desperate to go back sometime soon to my old stomping ground, Govan.

As a psychic, I find it's nigh on impossible to do readings for family and close friends – for some reason the information just doesn't come through the way it normally should when I read for someone close and if it does come through at all it's usually quite iffy and the accuracy can be, to say the least 'off target' a bit. So, a long time ago I decided that I'd never attempt to psychically read anyone close to me again. Well, I wonder if the area I lived in around Langlands Road and the distant memories of my childhood visitors are all still too close to me even now? Maybe some things in our past are supposed to remain there, buried in time. After all, every experience we have in this, our physical lives, makes us who we are but I still remain optimistic that one day I may see those entities again and find out why they chose me.

I often wonder if Andrew and the other two children are still there, remaining forever young as they watch the physical world they once briefly lived in, dying and being reborn or rebuilt again? I'm a rational enough person to wonder to myself if maybe they were all simply figments of a young, fertile imagination – sometimes better known as imaginary friends. Or could it be that they just didn't recognise or trust some strange fully grown man who was standing in the street with his eyes closed (and looking like a right big numpty!) attempting to communicate with the dead on that cold February day? I will be back there again one day to try again but for now I hope those wee souls are at peace . . . wherever they may exist.

3

GALLUS GHOST HUNTERS AND GRAVEYARD VIGILS

For any readers out there who are planning to spend their future nights in our wee country's draughty, haunted locations, I salute you. The pursuit of ghosts and spirits is definitely not a pastime for the faint-hearted and takes both courage and a little bit of ingenuity to do correctly.

Anyone can stand in a creepy location at 2 a.m. asking for proof of spirit but, to be able to catch real evidence, the experienced investigator needs many tools of the trade at his or her disposal.

In private locations, where someone has asked for help and wants their privacy respected, a notepad or dictaphone is usually sufficient for me because no other proof is needed for anyone involved in the invest, but for people or groups who wish to document their paranormal evidence, there are many tools – both scientific and traditional – that can be used to hunt ghosts. The following list, although not exhaustive, will give you an insight into what is needed as you enter the world of paranormal investigation.

Most groups use the traditional skills of mediums and psychics to attempt to access information, as well as more scientific methods such as EMF detectors. These detectors can pick up electrical fields over many different frequencies and when any disruption is registered it could mean some possible paranormal activity is happening. I say 'possible' activity because I've seen many false alarms when these meters are used by inexperienced investigators. It has to be said that they are very sensitive instruments and can give the impression that a spirit is in front of you when in fact it is something as natural as a power cable or a light socket that could be causing the disturbance. For this reason, I'd always advise any users to treat the readings on an EMF detector with the utmost scepticism until all other possibilities have been checked. Most experienced investigation groups do some baseline tests before an invest earlier in the day so that any natural sources of electricity can be located and disregarded as paranormal during the evening. I really like EMF detectors though and when used properly they can give some very interesting results that occasionally validate the information a psychic feels in certain haunted areas, such as the experience we had at Govan Old Parish Church graveyard, where the reading on Tom M's EMF detector matched my own connection with spirit.

Another favourite with serious ghost hunters I know is an infrared thermal scanner. These devices are excellent for pinpointing a cold spot in a room or even outside and can give fascinating results. I've seen several spirit entities on invests and when the scanner was used the temperature was significantly different in that area – great stuff and well worth buying for anyone serious about finding evidence of the paranormal.

One of the most useful tools I've seen used is a simple digital or tape recorder. These are invaluable for picking up any EVP recordings (Electronic Voice Phenomena). The usual routine when searching for EVP is for a member of the group to ask questions and simply press the record button. When the recording is played back at a later date and enhanced, occasionally there can be some convincing evidence that *something* seems to have answered back. However, I've listened back to thousands of EVP recordings that sound like simple static noise to me whilst other people present have made out words. It's always wise to remember that the brain naturally tries to look for some sense in chaos and can make us think we are hearing words or seeing visions when there is nothing there. Some people even believe EVP phenomena are caused by alien contact or psychic echoes emanating from the actual person who was recording the EVP at that moment. Others, including myself, believe that very rarely we do manage to catch a glimpse of the other side through this kind of recording. Always remember, however, that the airwaves are filled with all kinds of signals; radios, mobile phones, television channels, walkie-talkies etc. I'd advise anyone listening back to EVP recordings to do so with a rational ear until you hear a definite answer to a question you have asked on the night or until you hear something clear and sensible that is related to your investigation. I've heard one or two amazing EVPs over the years but have to say that probably eighty per cent of the evidence seems to consist of scratchy electric noises that have made no sense to me personally – although many others would disagree. EVPs are a very interesting part of paranormal investigating though and well worth trying out . . . you might get a real surprise when they answer you.

While investigating any large place it's always handy to have some motion detectors placed in different areas. I believe these gadgets are invaluable on an invest because they pick up any signs of movement in a part of a location while the rest of the team are elsewhere. I remember one frightening experience I had a while back with detectors which convinced me of their effectiveness. I was sitting with an investigator in a dark corridor of a deserted asylum at around 1 a.m. (as you do). Suddenly we heard the sound of loud, heavy footsteps starting at the end of the corridor. As the footsteps slowly seemed to make their way towards us, the two motion detectors which were placed about ten feet away were set off and the activity stopped instantly. To me, this was definite proof that these devices are invaluable for ghost hunting and I think investigators should use them in larger paranormal sites. Occasionally animals and rodents can set them off of course, but overall I think they're a great addition and the sound of them picking up some movement in the dead of night in a distant empty room or corridor while everyone is accounted for creates a real sense of excitement and fear that certainly wakes the assembled group up in the wee small hours!

When you think of any TV programme on the paranormal, you will have noticed how the stars make their way through various haunted houses and inns with a hand-held camera practically stuck up their noses. You may also have noticed how they always film in night vision too which means they can capture any possible phenomena in the dark (and it looks creepy for the telly). A night-vision camera is a great piece of equipment to use and video footage is probably the best kind of proof available to convince anyone of paranormal activity – after all, to see something in front of your own eyes is fine but to be able to film it and be able to play it back to others for their opinion is a great feeling.

Night-vision cameras pick up dust particles or flying insects very easily though and these can be misinterpreted as 'spirit orbs', so, as ever, I'd advise you to look at any footage rationally and examine every detail because there is so much dust in old buildings that can be disturbed when people are walking around. Throughout the last few years there has been some interesting footage caught on night vision cameras by many groups but nothing strong enough to convince hardened sceptics yet. Who knows what the future might bring though.

This might sound obvious but a couple of photographic cameras are needed when investigating. Tom M, a very experienced investigator I've worked with (who I mentioned in the previous chapter), always likes to have both a digital and 35mm film camera on him when ghost hunting. He says, 'Digital cameras are fine for catching orbs but using a film camera gives a more realistic view of the area in question. I think orbs should be disregarded as proof of spirit now and we should be searching for full apparitions in photographs as proof of life after death.'

There are countless 'ghost' photographs on the internet but with the advent of advanced computer editing programs being available on most PCs, the validity of many of these images is, to say the least, questionable. Still, it's always handy to have some cameras – along with plenty of extra batteries! The presence of spirit seems to drain equipment quickly for some reason.

I always like to take an old-fashioned thermometer with me to investigations. I find electric thermometers tend to go a bit haywire when spirit is close by, but mercury thermometers never let me down and always give a good indication of alterations in temperature. Sometimes the traditional methods seem to work better in active areas but it's all a matter of opinion and choice. I've touched on some of the modern day technical gadgets that can be used to hunt for ghosts but what about the age old techniques that have been used for centuries? Opinion is divided of course but some people swear by them and continue to disregard the modern high-tech instruments. As I said already, it's up to each individual and his or her belief system. For instance, someone of a scientific mind would never use dowsing-rods because they've never been scientifically proven to be accurate but, throughout the years, I've met some people who dowse and they have delivered some amazing results in my view.

Dowsing consists of the person – or 'dowser' – holding bent rods in both hands and walking around areas until the two rods seem to move towards or away from each other involuntarily. Some people say this movement is caused by small involuntary muscular contractions called 'ideomotor responses' and I tend to agree. However, in my opinion, that doesn't mean the movement is not caused by psychic phenomena. I think it's simply the subconscious relaying the information to the dowser and his or her muscles then moving accordingly. Some of you may have seen people dowsing for water on TV but I believe it also has a very important place in attempting to seek spirit.

Another traditional method I've seen is the use of wind chimes. Some investigators place them in rooms or areas in the hope that a passing spirit will cause a draught and make them chime. It doesn't take a degree to figure out that you *must* place them somewhere where there is absolutely no chance of a draught or breeze – only then will they be of any use. Now, let me say that having lived in this windy wee country all my life, I think it's very rare to find somewhere without a wee draught! So be extremely careful where you set wind chimes up as they can cause the group a lot of pointless running to and fro if they start chiming because of a sneaky draught that you missed earlier!

Now I'm going to talk about the most controversial tool used in investigations: the communication board. I've personally witnessed several occasions where people have used a board 'for a laugh' and ended up with deep psychological problems or, even worse, spiritual problems. I always use the analogy that making an unprotected communication through these instruments is the spiritual equivalent to leaving your front door ajar all night – you may be lucky and some decent person will come along and close it for you, but chances are some shady character will sneak through the door and goodness knows what could happen. Well, the unprotected use of one of these boards is the same. So, although the dead usually won't harm us, we have to remain careful and safe at all times . . . because evil does exist over there too.

For those of you who haven't seen a communication board, it is basically a board with letters and numbers written on it and a 'yes' and 'no' at either end. The board is placed on a table or other flat surface and the people sitting around the board hold on to a planchette. This is usually a smaller triangular board – sometimes on casters – which the spirit entities allegedly guide towards each letter or number spelling out dates and words etc. relating to questions asked by members of the group. Sometimes an upturned glass is used instead of a planchette, usually with similar results.

Most sessions I've seen involve the people around the board moving it either involuntarily or fraudulently. But, very occasionally, some of the information given has been fascinating and I'm sure was from the psychic realm. Once or twice I've actually seen the glass move itself and spell out *me* and *hi* but ninety-nine per cent of the time, I believe the living are responsible for the messages, consciously or not. This can still cause some problems though and, no matter how sceptical the sitters are, they should *always* protect themselves and ask their guides for protection . . . go on, just do it to keep this auld psychic happy. Or better still, don't dabble at all!

I imagine any cynics reading this will scoff at my last statement but in my time I have seen rational, sane individuals become deeply affected by the messages that can appear in front of their eyes. I genuinely think some forms of spirit contact, for instance boards like this, are psychologically damaging to certain people and should be avoided. They do, however, seem to give instant results and therefore have been used for centuries by people attempting to receive after-death communication and I'm sure they'll be in circulation for a long time after we all leave this physical world.

These boards tend to fascinate young people in particular and on occasion can mess their heads up. One particular story I know very well concerns three young boys and I'll tell you about it next – the question is, did the communication board they used foretell the tragedy that befell them or did they follow some self-fulfilling prophecy caused by it? You can make your own mind up.

What follows is a true story about the darker side of communication boards. This is the reason why I'm wary of using them without protection and guidance and an insight into the kind of 'visitors' who can appear during a session. It's entirely up to you, the reader, to believe it or not.

In the early '80s, three bored, drunken teenagers used a home-made communication board for fun one night and as they sat in the woods drinking cheap beer, they continuously asked and taunted the spirits to respond. The faint light of their fire and the bright moon illuminated the handwritten letters and numbers in the centre of the group, as well as their hands and the glass they had placed their fingers on. At the beginning of their 'fun' the results were, to say the least, laughable. Most of the 'messages' were insults aimed at each member – definitely not from the hands of a spirit. After some persuading, one of the youths who was known to be 'a bit strange' asked in earnest and with some respect for a connection . . . there was nothing. One of the other boys asked again – this time the glass began to move slowly amid accusations from each of the boys that one of the others was controlling it. Suddenly, 'Dead boy' began to communicate. They all gasped and stared at each other with a mixture of disbelief and suspicion. 'Dead boy' told the group through the board that he was a teenage merchant seaman who was murdered in the early twentieth century and wanted to exact his revenge on all concerned. As the three youths laughed nervously and drank more beer, 'Dead boy' began to write very personal messages about each person in the group, messages they definitely didn't want each other to see and each was sure the other two had absolutely no way of knowing in advance.

As the laughter began to fade to gasps of embarrassment and fear, the lad who was 'a bit strange' knew that the trio were dabbling with something very dangerous. He suggested the session must end immediately but still the other two continued and said he was a coward for leaving the circle. After hesitating for a moment he took another drink of beer and placed his finger back on the glass as it glided across the board. 'Dead boy' welcomed him back and began to spell chilling messages for each of the group. He told the 'strange' youth he would be haunted for the rest of his life by the dead and would end up in an insane asylum by the age of thirty. He told the other two they would never reach thirty and would take their own lives in a haze of drink and drugs. It was at that moment the 'strange one' of the group lifted the board and threw it into the fire then smashed the glass. As they sat and drank themselves into oblivion that summer evening they tried to forget 'Dead boy' and the chilling messages he gave each of them. After all, they were young and felt they were going to live forever and didn't believe in all that rubbish.

As the sun rose at dawn they all staggered home and didn't really speak about their strange experience to each other again. And as we all know life takes us on many different roads and the three youths soon lost touch.

It was many years later when one of the group was walking along Argyle Street in Glasgow that he heard a familiar voice from the crowd shouting his name: it was a brother of one of the group, who gave him the terrible news. His old friend had committed suicide a few years before. As the hairs stood on the young man's neck he asked hesitantly about his other old friends and dropped into the conversation a question about the welfare of the other member of the group from that evening. This friend too had died by his own hand in a grubby London bed-sit many years earlier. It seemed 'Dead boy's' premonitions had come true. But then again, the survivor wasn't insane as the spirit had foreseen and had never needed medical help with his mental health! So it didn't all come true . . . or did it?

After a few minutes of idle chitchat they both said their goodbyes and went their separate ways. As the 'strange' one walked along the busy street, holding back his tears, he felt a deep sense of sadness at the loss of two of his childhood acquaintances and felt a little scared for his own sanity. As the tears finally began to roll down his face he walked up the stairs into a little room, sat down, prepared himself for his next client and looked at the other side of the table; several people were standing in line desperately waiting to talk to their loved ones. He wiped the tears from his eyes, smiled at them and asked if they could please rest for a while and he would attempt to help them over the next few hours. The assembled group then evaporated in front of his eyes. His first living client then walked through the door and sat down desperate to speak to the 'strange' guy who is haunted daily by the dead . . . I'll let you decide who the strange guy is.

If you decide that a communication board would be a tool you'd like to use on investigations then you must protect yourself well – even if you don't believe in people like me, just humour me because it isn't worth it. There are many evil entities that will come through if they get the chance and even if they don't there are many disturbing psychological issues that can be created through these boards. I guess it's up to every individual but at least I warned you of the dangers and maybe you can avoid them. If you have decided on a communication board then good luck – you'll need it.

A good idea on any investigation is to use a trigger object, which can be anything really. Most groups use a coin or something similar and place it on a piece of paper. Then the shape of the coin is carefully traced onto the paper and both the coin and paper are left in a closed-off room and checked later to see if there has been any movement. Other variations of this involve placing talcum powder on a surface in a sealed-off area and checking later for any sign of ghostly handprints. There are many different ways of placing trigger objects in haunted places, but you have to make sure there is absolutely no chance of fraud or trickery, so it's best to place them in a locked room. Only then can you be certain that the results have been caused by paranormal interference.

The usual routine a group goes through to organise an investigation takes weeks, sometimes months. Firstly, there's the difficult task of obtaining permission to get into the location in the first place. Pubs are usually OK because most landlords are quite happy to find out what's going on in their premises or don't really care and are happy for the publicity, but councils on the other hand can be tricky – there's usually so much red tape involved that some of the best haunted locations in the country haven't been investigated yet. I think this is a shame but that's the way it is.

Once the location is chosen and permission is granted, a date is set and the group, which can consist of anything between two and twenty members, prepares for the night. Usually, on arrival, everyone is given their tasks and then the real excitement begins. I've been at several places where absolutely nothing has happened but, as I've already said, you can't make the spirit people perform and it really is a game of chance sometimes. One paranormal group I know of had phenomenal activity in a famous pub while another a few months later got absolutely nothing. I believe that the people present can stir up activity too, albeit unconsciously. For instance, one night I was involved in a communication board session in an old castle (the name of which I won't disclose) but whenever the grumpy security guard came near, everything ceased. Mind you, he was a scary character – that's why I'll keep the name of the castle a secret!

What I'm trying to say here is that some people seem to dampen the energy in an area, while others, like me, seem to unconsciously cause activity.

When people see haunted investigation programmes on the TV they forget that what they are witnessing are all the juicy bits. If you go on any investigation, be prepared for long periods of standing about in the dark, waiting for something to occur.

I think psychics and mediums can be a great addition to any team but have to say that any information we relay should be thoroughly checked. I once saw a young female 'psychic' at one location who told many horrific, grizzly tales of murder, deceit and corruption that allegedly took place forty years before. The poor owner of the place was horrified at the nonsense she was hearing about her not-so-distant ancestors and everything the girl said was disputed by the whole family involved. An uncomfortable scene ensued. I believe that it's better to say nothing when you have nothing to say. This girl also told a young guy he was being possessed by an evil spirit when he was actually suffering an asthma attack that night. But, I must say, someone like that is rare and I've also been witness to the unearthing of some great information when a psychic receives a strong connection at a scene. Alongside scientific methods, the info can be fascinating and I think adds to the overall excitement of the evening.

My first personal paranormal 'investigation' actually began as a dare one night many years ago. I was on a night out in the Merchant City area of Glasgow and a friend of mine bet me £20 I couldn't sit in the Necropolis at the stroke of midnight for half an hour. I rose to the challenge and so at 11.50 p.m. we made our way up to the dark gates of the place. I went in alone with my pals sniggering behind me and walked up the dark winding pathway that was lined with huge gravestones and statues. I have to admit I was terrified, but not of the dead. I was scared in case any mad axe-men or lunatics were in the place as my pals' sniggers faded into the distance.

At the top of the hill which the graveyard is built on, the crypts and tombs are a sight to behold – Glasgow's richest people were buried here many years ago and the ornamental artwork and gothic atmosphere is wonderful to behold.

I sat myself down beside a large tomb and stared at the clear, moonlit sky above me. When I realised no other living soul was about I knew this was going to be an easy twenty quid for a poor student like me.

I must have been there for about fifteen minutes or so when I heard a female voice quietly singing. I thought I'd been joined by some drunken woman at first, but when I listened closely the solo voice was beautiful and the song was not recognisable to me. I quietly placed myself between two large tombs so as not to be seen and watched to find out who this was. As the singing became louder, I still couldn't see a soul anywhere and decided to blow my cover and have a look.

I finally stepped out from my hiding place and saw one of the most beautiful young women I'd ever seen standing at a grave with little flowers in her hands (I think they were daisies). She was bare-footed, wore a long white shroud or gown and had long dark hair that went all the way to her waist. As I stood there transfixed by her image and the sound of her voice, she turned and looked at me with a surprised expression on her face then promptly ran away. I quickly followed her through the cemetery until she smiled at me and disappeared at a gravestone a few hundred yards away. I was still not sure if she had been alive or in spirit at this time and made my way out of the place quite puzzled – but still collected my twenty quid!

Back home I just couldn't get her out of my head all week, so (stupidly) I decided to return the next weekend alone to the same spot at the same time.

This time I bought her a rose from a vendor on the way there just to show her I meant no harm. I was intrigued and wanted to find out more. So after a bit of searching, I made my way up to the same tomb and sat down on the damp grass . . . but there was nothing. An hour passed and not a peep. I then became sure she had indeed been some strange *living* person who may have been frightened by a big long-haired (at that time) bloke appearing out from between two huge gravestones! I wondered what someone would be doing alone in a graveyard in the wee small hours. How weird, I thought. (Pot calling the kettle black I think.) After a while in the freezing cold, I finally decided to make my way back to the hustle and bustle of the city, feeling a wee bit embarrassed and disappointed by this time.

I had managed to forget all about my night there until a year or so later when I passed the place one winter afternoon. I felt a strange compulsion to visit the same area in daylight so I took a detour and yet again walked into Glasgow's 'City of the Dead'. By that time I'd forgotten where I'd seen her and the rows and rows of large tombs and crypts were quite confusing and made me lose my bearings for a moment. Then suddenly I followed my instincts and found the tomb I'd sat at before. I was surprised to see the rose I'd brought the last time, all withered and dead, but the package it was sold in was still perfect. I paused for a moment as the wind whistled around me, paid my respects to everyone buried in the area (I always believe we must show respect to the dead in graveyards) and smiled to myself and began to walk away. After only a few steps I distinctly heard the same voice in the wind, singing the same song again but when I turned and looked around, there was absolutely no sign of her anywhere. I definitely felt her presence strongly around me though but was disappointed not to see her vision again. I bent down and noticed something beside the faded rose on the ground – a wee bunch of picked dead daisies lay beside the rose. I thanked her out loud and the singing slowly faded away.

Was it the spirit girl who placed them there? Or was it just some coincidence that someone else placed the little wild flowers beside the rose? I guess you'll have your own theory but me . . . well, let's just say that all these years later, I visit the same spot annually and leave a rose for the shy spirit lassie who loved to sing.

It is an amazing feeling to see (and possibly) interact with spirit the way I did all those years ago in that graveyard and many other times since in various locations. However, I only saw that spirit girl once again after that day – about three years after the first communication – and her apparition seemed rather faint and blurred, I have to say. I still don't know her name or anything about her but I suppose that's the beauty and enjoyment of investigating the paranormal; sometimes the medium is overwhelmed with the amount of information received and other times he is left puzzled like everybody else. That's what drives me, and I imagine others, to push the boundaries of after-death communication and continue to investigate the elusive spirit world. I believe that if we did know all the answers then no doubt people's interest would wane. After all, the chase is always better than the catch they say . . . but I think we've a long way to go before that day comes and until then many dedicated individuals will keep searching for definite proof that life does go on.

4

FACE TO FACE WITH AN ABERDEEN POLTERGEIST

It must seem very strange to the casual observer to imagine any sane person spending their evenings walking through deserted old locations, usually in complete darkness, searching for signs of ghostly activity while analysing in detail the slightest bump or creak as a possibility of communication from discarnate spirits. But across the world many rationally minded – and very normal – individuals have decided to give up their free time (and sleep) to search the numerous alleged haunted locations that are all around us and attempt to find conclusive proof that everlasting life does exist in some form.

As I stated in the last chapter, many new paranormal investigation groups have sprung up all over the place and I believe that it definitely is a case of the more groups there are, the more chance there is of finding good evidence. But ghost hunting is by no means a recent pastime. In fact, one of the oldest investigation groups in the UK began in the mid-nineteenth century and still visits many paranormal sites throughout the British Isles to this day. An excellent Scottish group I know are called Paranormal Investigation Scotland. They have been dedicating themselves to finding the truth for many years and are one of the longest running groups in the country. They have some excellent footage and reports of many Scottish hauntings on their website that make fascinating reading. The team have spent evenings in every kind of location imaginable, from creepy castles, ships and jails to private homes. When questioned as to why they have decided to dedicate their time and effort to searching the country for proof of spirit, Team Leader, Alex says, 'We conduct paranormal investigations to seek knowledge from spirit and to use that knowledge in order to advise, assist and help any spirit or living person who may need help, advice or assistance.'

With people as thorough and devoted to seeking the truth as Alex and the team, I hope maybe one day soon, with the help of the latest technology, Paranormal Investigation Scotland and the other groups dotted around the country will capture that definitive piece of proof that is needed to show everyone, once and for all, that we do exist after the death of the physical body.

It's only natural to imagine an old deserted asylum or a dilapidated castle having some ghostly inhabitants and there are many stories of encounters with the dead at locations like these to merit investigating further. Surprisingly, two of the most terrifying investigations I have personally encountered didn't occur in some scary place that had grizzly historic stories attached – the hauntings happened in the least likely of places. One was in a private house and the other in a renovated guesthouse. Both were owned by two normal everyday families. All of the lovely people involved have kindly allowed me to tell their stories here in the hope that others suffering the same problems with a haunted house may be able to realise that they are not alone in the world and that there are alternative ways to deal with such a problem once all possible rational explanations have been exhausted. I have changed names and addresses to protect their identity.

Private Investigation 1: Aberdeen
It was 11 p.m. when I opened the first email.

Dear Tom,

Please help us. We are at our wits end and have barely slept for months. Myself, my husband and my young daughter moved into our house last summer and things were fine for the first while, apart from the usual bangs and bumps, which we put down to central heating, but recently there have been definite footsteps on the stairs and several times I've seen figures walking around in the hall. Our cooker turns itself on and the furniture gets thrown around while the house is empty – so much so that we thought we'd been burgled once.

I had the place blessed by a local priest last month but it seems that things have gotten much worse since that day. Even my husband, who is a complete sceptic to all this stuff, admits to being woken at night by the bumps and noises downstairs (which sound like voices sometimes) and occasional growling sounds in the room.

Our eight-year-old daughter sleeps beside us now because her face and legs have been scratched while she slept and her bed was being continually shaken by some unseen force.

This is destroying our lives Tom, you are our only hope. Please help us if you can.

Janet (pseudonym)

Every week my email inbox is filled with people asking for my help in some way and sadly I just can't manage to help everybody. For some reason, though, I felt drawn towards this case – even though Aberdeen is a fair distance from where I live. So, after a few weeks of emails and phone calls I decided to head up there and find out who, or what, was causing their problems.

The family didn't like the idea of a large group turning up on their doorstep with ghost-hunting equipment and asked if I could either come alone or with another person. So a date was set and I prepared to make the journey to the Granite City by myself . . .

A week later as I sat on the train to Aberdeen on a rainy Monday morning, I gazed through the carriage window at the countryside outside. Through the droplets of water that ran down the other side of the glass intermittently, the scene was reminiscent of some monochrome picture, mainly due to everything looking so grey and drab, but for some reason I really appreciated the strange beauty of this wet and windy homeland of mine through that rain-soaked steamed-up window. After a while my mind drifted back to my past; I could never have imagined in my wildest dreams that my future life's work would be so strange and controversial. Here I was, on my way to a location to attempt to communicate with something that many people say doesn't exist, by using a means of communication and senses that some people say don't exist – I wish I'd taken woodwork at school!

I finally reached my destination a few hours early and proceeded to take a stroll around the city centre for a couple of hours in the rain, visiting alleged haunted places. I love to do that wherever I go. As I walked through the wet, reflective streets I took time to admire the elegant granite buildings surrounding me and I tried to get a feel for this city and its people before the investigation began. Some of the places I visited that day were very interesting and are included in the Psychic Tourist chapter further on in this book. A few hours later Janet picked me up at the train station and we then drove for a while to the family home which was located on the outskirts of the city. Janet was in her mid twenties and on first appearances seemed a very sensible lassie. I could see immediately that she was extremely tense, tired and sick of the whole experience she was going through. Her eight-year-old daughter stared at me from the back seat all through the journey with a mixture of apprehension and puzzlement. Janet told me her husband, Jim (pseudonym), was waiting at the house for us and apologised for him in advance as he was extremely wary of my visit because he really 'hated' psychics. This made me feel a wee bit cautious of our meeting to say the least – I can handle troublesome spirits a lot easier than 'psychic haters'.

It was late afternoon by the time we arrived at their home – a nineteenth-century converted gatehouse that was surrounded by trees and shrubs. The elegant driveway and gardens that led to the front porch of the house were beautiful to look at and the entire picture in front of my eyes was that of an idyllic family abode. Even in the pouring rain with the dark skies above, the place had a real air of elegance and must have been an irresistible purchase in the previous summer months for the couple.

Jim opened the door, smiled and shook my hand firmly. I'm glad to say I didn't get any sense of negativity or hate at all from him and must admit I was extremely relieved at being welcomed so warmly. When we entered the hallway of the house I was surprised to experience . . . absolutely nothing! Not one single spirit or entity was present in the place. Was my journey to Aberdeen a complete waste of time, I asked myself. Maybe these people were imagining it all? Maybe they were simply 'over imaginative' and delusional? I usually pick something up in the residual energy of a place as soon as I walk in but this time, psychically speaking, it was as flat as a pancake. I'd say a very large percentage of private haunted investigations I'm invited to turn out to be all down to people's imagination – was this another one?

After a quick tour of the house the three of us sat in the kitchen and had a few cups of coffee. I still sensed nothing paranormal in the place and when Janet was talking about the alleged activity that was happening, Jim would smile cynically and glance at her. She would then glare back at him and continue her conversation with me, creating a very uncomfortable atmosphere all around. It didn't take a qualification in psychology to see that this marriage was reaching breaking point and they needed help of some sort, but maybe not from someone like yours truly. After a half hour or so I began to think Jim may have been correct and Janet may have been imagining things after all.

This scenario continued for a while until Janet left the room for a moment and I was left alone with Jim.

I took a sip of coffee smiled at him and said, 'Listen Jim, I've come all the way from Glasgow, I've given up my time to help you guys here and I'm doing all this out my own pocket. If there aren't any ghosts here there's nothing I can do to help ye. So if ye want I'll just go back home.'

He paused for a moment and then, much to my surprise, burst into tears. 'There is something strange going on in this house, Tom. I try and keep strong for Janet and my wee girl by pretending I don't believe in it all . . . but I've seen things and heard things in here that I never would've believed six months ago. We need help mate.'

I paused for a moment because I genuinely didn't know what to say to him. There was obviously *something* going on in this house to cause this distress but at that moment I thought I could do nothing at all to help the situation. Was this some form of group hypnosis and was Jim simply being carried along in the hysteria created by Janet? – I'd seen that happen many times before in supposed haunted places. As I was about to question him further there was a sudden sound of loud footsteps directly above us. I didn't think anything strange in this at first until Janet came running in to the kitchen with their little girl and I realised it wasn't them!

'That's it starting again,' Janet said to Jim as she placed the earphones of her iPod on to little Mia.

Jim stared at me helplessly as the heavy thumping upstairs continued. At that moment I realised this was no imagination or group hysteria and had to admit it did sound like definite footsteps. I knew that something strange was causing that noise in the room upstairs.

'Have you had the central heating checked recently?' I asked.

'It's working perfect Tom . . . I'm a plumber to trade,' Jim replied.

Couldn't argue with that then. After a few moments the footsteps seemed to make their way across the upstairs floor towards the upper landing and stairs and it sounded as if whatever was causing the noise now seemed to be making its way down the stairs one by one towards us. This was a regular occurrence they informed me.

Jim pulled Janet and little Mia close to him in the corner as I stood in the middle of the kitchen listening to the approaching noise. The sound of every descending step creaking under the strain of a mysterious invisible force was very eerie to say the least.

I quickly walked out into the dimly lit hall and the sound instantly ceased – I think it was around the fifth step from the bottom. Although I wasn't 100 percent certain that something ghostly was there with me, I was now convinced this was not dodgy central heating. As the air around me grew colder and colder I began to realise something was watching my every move in that hall. It seemed that whatever this was, it liked to play games with the living and I was its newest adversary.

'Who are ye and what do ye want?' I asked out loud.

Even I can see how ridiculous it must seem to picture a grown man standing in a dark hall shouting at an empty staircase, but I knew for certain that there was some kind of entity present that evening and I was convinced it could hear every single word I said.

I'm not sure if it was my eyes playing tricks in the twilight but I thought I saw a faint smoke-like substance quickly rising from the staircase towards the upper floor, but I couldn't be positive. I then felt nothing again . . . I was standing there all by myself and my invisible opponent seemed to have gone back to wherever it came from.

As I returned to the kitchen Jim stared at me nervously.

'Do ye think ye could help us here then Tom?' he asked.

'I'll try my best,' I replied. 'The problem is I don't know who or what it is that's doing this.'

It was then that Jim dropped the bombshell on me.

'We were thinking Tom . . . would ye mind if we spent the night at Janet's mammy's house tonight and we could leave ye here to find out?'

I was astonished and, for once, was lost for words.

'We just need a sleep . . . we'll pay ye whatever ye want, Tom,' Janet said as she held her husband's hand tightly.

I sat down at the table and took a drink of my now cold coffee.

'Well, I better get some caffeine in me. I think it's gonnae be a long night,' I replied with some trepidation in my voice.

Jim pulled out a bundle of twenty pound notes from his wallet and I gestured for him to put them back. No amount of money would have made me stay the night in that place alone – but my pigheaded stubbornness (and my stupidity!) would have. I was going to find out what was causing this trouble, and it seemed I was now doing it all by myself.

My night in Aberdeen was going to become a lot more interesting . . . and one of the most frightening experiences of my life.

As the family were about to drive off for the night, Jim promised to return at 7 a.m. and check to see how things were going. They both hugged me and, as I watched the tail-lights of their car disappear into the darkness, I took the time to stand for a moment, take a breath and get ready for the battle ahead. When I investigate the paranormal, I usually jot down some notes for my own reference. Below are the notes I took for my own personal records that night. They are practically unedited.

8.10 p.m.
I am now in the house alone and have been sitting in the lounge watching the TV and waiting for any disturbance. A few moments ago there was a loud crash from upstairs. I ran up to discover my bag, which I had left in the family guest room, was lying on the floor with all the contents spilled. I was sure I had left it securely on the bed earlier. I wonder to myself if this is coincidence or phenomena? I can pick up no presence though so probably not paranormal.

9.20 p.m.
The footsteps have begun upstairs again. I'm checking to see if they follow the exact same pattern as earlier. If so, there has to be some rational explanation for all this, for instance, timber expanding or constricting during certain time periods? It definitely seems as if someone heavy is stomping around with hobnail boots on directly above me! I have to go up and confront this thing now, whatever it is . . .

9.45 p.m.
Back in lounge again. Feeling a wee bit spooked now which is unusual for me. Just been up the stairs and as I walked into the bedroom above (the location of the footsteps) I am sure I fleetingly saw something large crouching in the corner. A distinct smell of body odour and vomit hit me as I entered that room; the smell was so strong I retched and had to cover my face. The sound of

footsteps instantly ceased again the moment I came in contact with the source. (How annoying!) I called out but received no communication. I honestly don't know what this is I'm dealing with. Hopefully I'll find out soon.

10.51 p.m.
Still in lounge. Things have been quiet the last while. Hearing the occasional shuffling sound directly outside the lounge door here – every time I look out there is nothing though and no sense of a presence near. Wonder if this thing is scared of me?

11.07 p.m.
Ignore the last thing I wrote – I'm definitely MORE scared of it! Whatever this thing is, it is getting very active and sounding a wee bit agitated now. Three loud thumps on the lounge door here, about a minute or so apart and there is now a distinct sound of dragging outside the lounge door right now! I need to get face to face with it so I'm opening the door . . .

11.19 p.m.
Can't believe this! I'm standing here in the lower hall in complete darkness trying to write this because all the lights in the house have just fused! Janet told me this happens regularly and electricians have checked them numerous times. This does not help my nervous state, believe me . . . footsteps above again! I'm sure I can hear heavy breathing this time coming from the landing above . . . maybe it's my breath though!!! Heart is racing, goose bumps all over . . . sweaty palms (why?) . . . bring it on!

Got my torch anyway but really need to find the electricity box now.

11.49 p.m.

Sure I saw a tall figure of a long-haired man moving across the top hallway into little Mia's bedroom! Stink hit me again. (Have they no deodorant in spirit world!) I got no response when I shouted after him.

Found electricity box but can't seem to get lights to work again – this is a nightmare!

I'm standing at the bottom of the staircase writing this and just noticed there is a woman silently staring at me from above – five or six stairs from the top . . . quite hard to see . . . dark clothes . . . hair tied up in a bun . . . eyes piercing . . . she's slowly coming down the stairs towards me . . .

12.20 a.m.

First time I've been scared by spirits for years! That scary looking woman on the stairs really frightened me. Embarrassed to say I ran into the lounge and shut the door on her! (What good will that do? – she's a ghost!) All quiet at the moment – got to get that fuse box fixed though.

12.53 a.m.

In kitchen at moment. Managed to get electricity back on (thank goodness). Fuse box is located under the stairs. While I was trying to fix it I heard several doors upstairs slamming shut and more footsteps on the staircase – could find no source of breeze or draughts to cause this. I'm SURE this is footsteps now. Definitely hearing heavy breathing sound outside door now . . . as usual, nothing there when I look – bored with this nonsense. They are playing games with me . . .

1.13 a.m.
Just visited toilet and handle was turned while I was inside. (Checked handle mechanism and it seemed fine.) Came downstairs and TV was turned on at full volume! Attempted communication but STILL nothing!!! Why won't they communicate? As I write this the lights have fused AGAIN! I'm scared to look but someone is standing directly behind me . . . don't think this is my mind playing tricks . . .

1.40 a.m.
Fixed lights and they instantly fused once again. In upper hall now, sitting in a chair by candlelight. I know they are around me now. Knocking sound on the bedroom door behind me – I refuse to be frightened by these buggers! The woman is showing herself to me again – directly in front of the flame of the candle . . . her face is crystal clear now . . . my hand is shaking here . . . she's staring directly into my eyes . . . even though she scares me I'm going to try and get some information from her. Heard a distinct 'Thomas' whispered from directly behind me – sounds masculine I think . . . can't write just now . . .

2.25 a.m.
I'm writing this as I sit on the outside porch of the house now. It's dark out here too. Thank goodness the rain has stopped for a while because I need a break from the phenomena I've just witnessed inside. When I asked the female why she was present in the house she silently

screamed in my face and her figure vanished. I still haven't found the answers I'm looking for in this house. Just noticed I have four deep scratches on my neck that are bleeding profusely . . . was it one of the spirits that hurt me? Or did I somehow unconsciously scratch myself? MUST remain rational. Whoever did it . . . it bloody hurts! . . .

Electric's still off and all lights are out – this is ridiculous. I REALLY don't want to go back in that dark evil house ever . . . rain just started again.

3.05 a.m.
Sitting in kitchen now . . . I'm leaving the fuse box as it is because it's taking too much time up and it would probably just go off again anyway. Heard my name being called from upstairs a while back but it's been silent here for a little while. The handle on the door is being rattled occasionally. Every time it happens it's making me jump out my skin! I'm attempting to communicate again but there's nothing! Something unusual and extremely disturbing has happened. I can't sense my spirit guides. This is not good!

3.27 a.m.
Still in kitchen. Was just about to write down here that all activity had stopped but as I put pen to paper there are definite heavy footsteps on the staircase again. My torch isn't working now because of a flat battery (Brand new battery in it today!) Only light source I have now is this rapidly burning candle. (I really hope it lasts.) Must admit I'm feeling extremely tense because I know the evil male spirit is outside the door waiting on me. (Why won't he

come in?) As I write this the door handle is now turning by itself and . . .

3.36 a.m.

Writing very shaky here . . . (hope I understand my own notes). Opened kitchen door and he's moved back on to the stairs, half way up . . . I'm genuinely terrified now . . . putrid smell is there again . . . he is now staring at me . . . must have been about six foot six when he was in his physical body . . . longish hair, balding and straggly sideburns . . . NEVER seen anyone look so wicked and I feel very threatened . . . my heart's racing . . . I don't like this, he's moving slowly down the stairs again . . . directly towards me . . .

3.38 a.m.

VERY disappointed in myself now – like a big Jessie I ran into the kitchen and closed the door when he approached me in the hall a few minutes ago . . . pull yourself together Tom! Just saw a female face looking in the window at me a moment ago – thought maybe Janet had returned but no such luck – it's the spirit woman again! Still here alone . . . (well kind of). Why did I agree to this!? Will never work as a psychic or medium again!

3.51 a.m.

Still in kitchen. I am now exhausted and strangely exhilarated. At this moment there is the sound of very light scratching on the other side of the kitchen door from me. I've had enough of this now! – I'm opening the kitchen door right now.

A minute has passed now . . . surprise surprise, there's nobody there . . . I'm jamming the door open with one of my shoes now . . . I'm going to have one last attempt at communication. Need an answer . . .

4.18 a.m.
Well, I'm outside again . . . in the middle of Aberdeen . . . I'm far away from home . . . in the rain . . . at a strange house . . . surrounded by trees . . . and bloody terrified. The nearest house looks quite far away – I could maybe walk there in ten minutes or so but what would the inhabitants think? How could I explain to them why I'm outside in the pouring rain, in the middle of the night, with one *******
shoe on!

Why am I out here?

Did some automatic writing earlier and kept getting the name 'Ross', date '1873' and the words 'YOU ALL PERISH' – charming. I then saw another apparition of the female spirit – this time she was hanging by the neck from the staircase. This has disturbed me greatly. I'm also feeling very sad for the poor soul. Didn't realise she had died like that.

From outside, I can hear what sounds like glass smashing inside the house now. Y'know something, I'm beginning to think this place should be razed to the ground. Am going to go back in and try some final prayers to attempt to help that poor female spirit move on . . . I feel so sad for her. I'm not even going to try with the big smelly ghost!

4.43 a.m.
Sitting in upper master bedroom. Couldn't find anything broken in the house but there WAS the sound of smashing earlier! Place is in complete darkness now because my wee candle's coughed its last I'm afraid.

Well, I asked the spirits to move on and said some prayers. Nothing happened for a while until I was shown a mental vision of the female spirit on her knees in prayer – then I was shown a beautiful bright light. I genuinely believe she has left this place.

Oh no, as I write this now there are heavy footsteps stomping around the ground floor . . . there is also the sound of doors opening and closing downstairs as if the male spirit is searching for something . . . this CAN'T be imagination!!!! I really hope it's not ME he's looking for . . . or could he be trying to find the woman? I now know her name was 'Alice' . . . she was a teacher who lived here once . . . who is this male though? I know she fears him but can't get more information . . . oh no . . . I can hear – and smell – him coming up the stairs now . . . time to run . . .

4.47 a.m.
Can't believe this . . . I'm hiding in the en suite bathroom now as I write this. He's upstairs somewhere now. Banging noises are coming from all around the top part of the house. To be honest, I'm sick and tired of all this! – NO MORE psychic work. Should I climb out of the window and run?

Haven't been scared of the dead for years so why now? Surely he can't harm me . . . what about scratched neck? Wait . . . footsteps moving towards this door . . . I'm trembling now . . .

5.10 a.m.
Still in en suite in complete darkness. Door is being hit now and then from other side . . . I've definitely heard my name being called out once or twice from downstairs – it

sounded like a child's voice but not sure. Pulled myself together now though and I'm ready for this eejit! He can bang and bump all he wants but I KNOW he can't hurt me! This is going to be the ultimate psychic 'square go' and I'm not going to run away! I just hope and pray my spirit guides (wherever they are) protect me from this entity.

Just thinking; if this is all in the imagination as the sceptics say, then I must be completely insane because I can see and hear the door in front of me being hit from the other side now! OK, enough, I'm opening the door . . .

6.24 a.m.

I'm outside again, the rain's stopped and the birds are now singing in the trees – I don't think I have ever been as tired as this in my life but I also feel elated.

Well, the male spirit made lots of noise around me but I just closed my eyes and constantly shouted for him to leave and kept praying out loud. After a half hour or so it all ceased and the house has become peaceful . . . I'm sure both spirits are gone now. The place seems fresh. Got the electric back on now and I'm nursing a much needed coffee. I still feel terrible for 'Alice' but I hope she can finally rest in peace beside her loved ones in spirit.

I hope Janet, Jim and little Mia can live their lives in peace now too.

Me? . . . I think it's time to give all this psychic stuff up and join the world of the living.

That afternoon as I travelled back home on the train, attempting to fight the overwhelming urge to drift off to sleep, I smiled to myself as we passed through the many rain-soaked landscapes once again. As the other passengers on board read their books or magazines and chatted to each other, none of them could possibly have imagined the strange and terrifying previous twenty-four hours the lone guy sharing the carriage with them had experienced.

The gentle rocking sound of the train, coupled with the extreme exhaustion I was overcome with caused me to close my eyes and gently drift off into a much needed sleep. It was then that I experienced a very vivid dream. In my dream, a young girl dressed in white walked towards me from a background of bright blue. She appeared to be in her early twenties and had beautiful long flowing dark hair and intense piercing eyes. A young, dark haired boy walked behind her, stopped at her side and took hold of her hand. It was then I recognised her as the lady I'd seen in the house the night before; it was 'Alice' but she now looked so much younger and happier looking, definitely not the frightening figure I'd witnessed the previous night. In the dream we were both wrapped in a deep sense of emotion as she smiled, reached out her hand to my face and opened her mouth as if to say something . . . it was at that precise moment that I was sadly woken up by some vigorous shaking.

'C'moan pal, ye canny bloody sleep here all day! Ye're at Glesga Central!' shouted the wee guard in my ear.

I was definitely brought back to earth with a bump! I mumbled a 'thank you' or something similar to him, picked up my bag and left the train. That vision of her face was embedded in my mind as I walked through the dark streets of Glasgow that evening though. I kept telling myself that it was 'only a dream' but still I saw her young face in front of my eyes as though carved forever in my memory. Who knows, maybe the dream on the train was just that – a dream. It was so vivid that it made me feel happy for her as I made my way home that evening. I never saw or dreamed about 'Alice' again but I sincerely hope she's at peace wherever she is. Possibly her spirit is finally side by side with the wee boy I saw holding her hand . . . I hope so.

And that was it. Thankfully, the family didn't experience any further activity after that and could finally live their lives in peace, in their beautiful home, which they still live in and have no intentions to move from at the moment.

I spoke to them before I wrote this and Jim told me that every single person who enters their house since my overnight visit always comments on the 'warm and inviting feeling' in the place. If only those people knew the hard work it took to create that feeling!

5

A GLASGOW FAMILY WHO WILL NEVER LEAVE

Private Investigation 2: Glasgow area

I first met John (pseudonym) after he came to me for a private sitting. He was in his early forties at the time and was a definite no-nonsense 'tell it like it is' character. So, when he came to me for the communication with his late father, who had passed some years earlier, I must say I found it one of the most difficult sessions I've ever experienced, due to his need for phenomenal accuracy and times and dates etc. If something didn't click with him there and then, he would give me a look as if to say 'Are you daft?' I guess I must have done OK in the end because his initial scepticism of my line of work was eventually replaced with a deeper fascination for life after death. To his business colleagues and staff, however, he has always maintained the persona of a cynical, hard-nosed businessman, fearing ridicule and losing his status as one of Scotland's toughest working-class entrepreneurs.

He visited me a couple of times after our first meeting and surprisingly, we began to get on extremely well, away from the psychic/client relationship.

I hadn't heard from him for a month or two when he called me up out of the blue one morning.

'Hello, Tom, it's me here – it's John,' he bellowed down the phone line.

'How are you doing, John?' I enquired.

'*You're* supposed tae tell *me* that, ya big dumpling!' he replied jokingly.

'I see you're still as sarcastic as ever! I guess you're doin' fine then,' I said as we both laughed.

After a few minutes conversation, he began to tell me the real reason he'd called me up.

'Remember during the last reading you saw me buying some land and building flats on it?' he asked.

I honestly couldn't remember, due to the fact that I very rarely remember anything that comes out in a reading with someone and have a very bad memory anyway.

'I don't remember that, John,' I answered.

'Well, ye did. So, anyway it all happened! Even down to the location,' he said.

'That's excellent mate,' I said as I quietly tried to jog my memory about telling him about the flats in the first place. 'So, what can I do for ye?' I asked.

'Well, here's why I'm phoning . . . ye didnae tell me the place would be haunted! A few of my workers have left the job sayin' they've seen somethin' or been slapped or kicked by somethin' invisible. Fancy comin' down and havin' a wee look?'

'No problem,' I replied. 'I've got a day off next week.'

'Next week! If I send a car over can ye make it here in an hour? I don't know what tae do. I really need help with this Tom.'

I could tell he was genuinely upset about the alleged activity in his building project and he is, after all, a very persuasive character! So I reluctantly agreed and within an hour and a half I was on site.

He had begun to build the flats on the site where an old derelict house had recently stood and by the look of things to my layman's eye all the work looked as if it was nearly done. I was promptly handed a hard hat and led into the building by John. The whole shell of the building had been built and all that remained to be done was to add the finishing touches to the job, for instance, the kitchen units etc. As soon as we entered the main entrance a cold chill ran down my spine. There was no heating in the building and the place was, of course, naturally a wee bit on the nippy side but this was the kind of chill I've felt many times before. This was a *supernatural* coldness – a deep sense that chills you to the bone instantly. It's hard to explain to anyone who has never experienced such a feeling but, believe me, it is a unique and unmistakeable sensation and it is one I do not like experiencing.

As I closed my eyes and began to tune in, John stared at me intensely, waiting for me to deliver some deep insight there and then.

'There are definitely some presences here,' I whispered quietly to him as I stared around the large foyer.

'I know that already! But who is it though? What is it? How many are there?' he asked impatiently.

I kept seeing a horrific vision of a woman killing a man by strangulation but could get no other information at that time, so I decided to keep the information to myself until I received definite contact.

'I'd need more time John,' I replied. 'Sometimes things don't come that easy.'

'It does for that psychic off the telly!' he snarled. 'Well, what about comin' back tonight then? Ye could do one of yer investigations,' he said as he leaned closer smiling.

'I can't, John.'

'Why?'

'I'm busy.'

'Doin' what? Watchin' the telly?' He grinned mischievously. 'Let me see . . . a hundred quid to yer favourite charity if ye do this for me.'

I paused for a moment. How many times does an offer like that come to the table? This was my only night off for the past few weeks and I had been looking forward to a night of relaxation. But the thought of turning down £100 for charity made me feel guilty so, after some deliberation, I decided to go for it, but not before trying to negotiate some more dosh for charity out of John

'OK, make it a hundred and fifty and I'll do it,' I said as he began to smile.

'Tell ye what, Tom, get rid of these spooks and we'll make it two hundred.'

We shook hands and he agreed to come collect me at 10.30 that night.

As planned, John arrived at my door on time and off we went, armed with torches, hard hats and my trusty pen and notepad so I could read back my notes the following day.

I have to be honest and say I really didn't feel like walking around a desolate work site and being in contact with spirit that evening and would have preferred to have chilled out in the land of the living, but I had made a promise and had to keep it, so an evening of reluctant ghost hunting lay ahead.

As we drove up to the work site, I couldn't help but notice how different the place seemed in the moonlight – it was probably due to the fact there was no lighting in the building or any *living* inhabitants. But I have to add, there seemed to be something strange about the location, something sinister . . . it was hard to pinpoint but . . . I felt nobody was welcome on this plot of land . . . especially me.

As John placed the key into the front entrance door, something metallic hit him on the back of the ear. I didn't see or hear it but John swore it was thrown from somewhere behind us and when we searched the ground around we found a nail lying close by. Did it fall from above and his imagination caused him to believe it was thrown? Well, as I've said many times before, it seemed very real to him.

As we walked into the dark building and simultaneously switched on our torches, the distinct shape of a tall male, wearing a hat of some description, was standing at the back doorway but quickly vanished. John, normally the bravest of people, screamed and pushed me in front of him.

'I saw a bloke there! Then he disappeared! That was the weirdest thing I've ever seen,' he screamed.

I knew there and then that someone was not happy about the building work going on and whoever this was would do anything to chase us out of there.

As we climbed the pitch-black stairs a small object flew directly past us from above and hit the wall to our right. On further inspection, we discovered it was another nail.

By this time John was shaking with fear.

'If they keep throwing nails at us like this, there'll not be enough left to finish yer building, John,' I whispered.

'I'm scared of nobody mate but all this spooky stuff is different. I hate tae think they can see me but I cannae see them,' John said as he lit up a cigarette with a trembling hand.

'Don't worry, they can't really hurt ye, John,' I whispered, trying to pacify my increasingly nervous co-investigator.

'Tell that tae my ear! I nearly got it pierced a minute ago,' he said.

As we were about to reach the top floor, something that sounded like a deep, gravelly voice resonated from somewhere in one of the flats above. Both of us were sure it said 'Get out!' which was promptly followed by yet another nail, or something similar, falling down the stairs. It was at that moment that John turned and ran!

'No way, I cannae dae this mate, sorry!' he shouted as he descended the stairs below me. 'I'll give ye extra tae yer charity big man, but I cannae dae this. This isn't right.'

'Come back for me in three hours than!' I yelled after him as the sound of the main door to the building slammed shut.

Here I was again, standing alone, in a dark, strange place, looking for dead people. 'Where did it all go wrong?' I asked myself. All of my friends were at home or in the pub having a quiet pint while I stood in this building surrounded by malevolent entities who would have liked nothing more than to physically harm me. But hey, I was there to do a job and I had to finish it . . . and if I succeeded I'd make sure a deserving cause got yet another £50.

Inside one of the vacant flats on the top floor, I was sure I could hear something moving around. At that stage I couldn't tell exactly where the sounds were coming from but I was desperate to find out where the voice we'd both heard a few moments earlier had emanated from so I continued up the last few stairs to the top.

I slowly entered the dark hall of the flat where I could hear the noise and nearly jumped out of my skin when a loud thump came from inside. No matter how many times I see or hear spirit, I still occasionally get a fright when I'm alone in the dark with them. I then heard the sound of children crying from somewhere in the house. I tried to be as rational as possible and questioned whether the children could have been outside in the street and the sound was travelling from there but I knew deep down it was coming from inside the building.

I decided to walk into the first flat I came to. As I sat on the floor for a moment and took a drink of water from my bottle, I was sure I caught a small figure out of the side of my eye. When I turned it was gone. Many people tell me this type of thing happens to them all the time and most of the time it can be attributed to a trick of the light but I was convinced I had a wee visitor in the room with me. So I decided to call out.

'Hello . . . I'm not here to harm ye but I'd appreciate it if ye could let me know who ye are. I can maybe try and help ye. Can ye bump the wall for me?'

There were two light bumps directly on the wall beside me.

'That's great. Thank you. Now could ye give me one bump for "yes" and two for "no" because I'd really like to talk with ye?'

One bump.

'Thanks. Are ye a boy?'

One bump.

'Well done pal. Do ye live here?'

One bump.

'Is there anybody else here with ye?'

One bump.

'I see . . . if ye can count can ye let me know how many others are here?'

Three bumps.

'Thank you. Is yer mummy and daddy here too?'

Two bumps.

'That's a shame. Do ye know where they are?'

Two bumps.

After a while, I managed to decipher his name as beginning with an 'F' and that he was scared of a female figure who seemed to be an aunt.

When the bumping noises ceased, I heard what sounded like a male voice in deep conversation somewhere downstairs, – I actually thought John had returned so I descended down the stairs. When I realised I was still 'alone' I sat on the bottom step, by now feeling disgruntled and a wee bit spooked. As usual in my private investigations, I began to write. What follows are my notes, more or less as they were written at the time:

11.42 p.m.

I'm sitting on the bottom step in the ground floor hall of the building. Apart from the place being very creepy and my eyes playing tricks in the darkness, I sense nothing . . . everything is really quiet now – there are occasional creaks and bumps but I am putting that down to the building settling . . . nothing paranormal to report at this moment since the communication upstairs and the mumbling voice down here a few minutes ago.

12.19 a.m.
Heard what sounded like a male coughing upstairs a moment ago. I checked and found absolutely nothing . . . no rough sleepers either as security is very tight on this building site . . . maybe sound travelling from outside? – I doubt it. Am back down on bottom step at moment and watching into rear garden area through door, where we saw an apparition of a male earlier when we entered the building at first . . . nothing to report though.

12.56 a.m.
Writing bit shaky . . . I am so excited . . . and privileged . . . outside the back door a male spirit figure has been playing around with two spirit children for the last minute or so – This is DEFINITELY not my eyes playing tricks! Makes me feel honoured to witness this . . . they look trapped in time . . . can't tell if children are boys or girls at moment . . . they can't see me at all and seem engrossed in their fun . . . male is about 40ish I think, dark haired, moustache, slim with a bunnet . . . think they've seen me now . . . oh no, children have vanished and male spirit doesn't look too happy . . . he's walking towards me . . .

1.04 a.m.
I'm on the upstairs landing now. Never ran so fast up three flights of stairs in my life. Am out of breath and heart is beating fast . . . very angry at myself for being a big feartie! Why am I here? The male spirit was playing with two kids

outside and when they noticed me watching through the glass of the back door downstairs, the children disappeared and the male turned and began to walk over to the back door directly at me! Like a big Jessie, I ran upstairs and now feel embarrassed at myself. As I stand up here looking down through the spaces I'm sure I can see a figure climbing up the stairs from the ground floor – is it my eyes playing tricks? The shadow has just reached the first floor of the building and . . . it's climbing the stairs again . . . it is making its way up to me . . . it's going to be up here in a moment . . . my eyes definitely aren't playing tricks!

At this stage I stood completely frozen while what can only be described as a 'shadowy figure' ascended the stairs towards me. I was scared but had to face whoever this was head on. As I waited with bated breath another object came whizzing past my head from behind and this was no nail! Whatever it was it missed me, hit the wall in front and rolled downstairs and seemed heavy – something was seriously trying to hurt me now. Finally, it appeared several steps below me – a dark mass with the vague features of a man – the same man from the garden. He stared up at me angrily.

'Who are ye?' I asked while every goose bump on my body rose.

'I'm Michael. Go away,' he replied in whispered tones.

'Why are ye throwing things at me, Michael?'

'Just leave . . . f**k off,' he answered.

'I haven't done ye any harm mate. Why are ye trying tae hurt me?'

He stared at me intently then his face contorted. 'Get out . . . get out . . . GET OUT!' he screamed over and over.

'Life goes on Michael! – You have to move on!' I screamed back.

He then flew past me at an incredible speed into one of the open doors behind. His energy made me feel as cold as ice. I began to write again.

1.31 a.m.

Lower hall area. The spirit that approached me on the stairs was definitely the male entity from the garden (Michael). He gave me some info but has now disappeared! I feel the back communal garden area is extremely active so am now on my way out to spend some time there.

1.56 a.m.

Standing in rear garden area. Sensing a lot of residual atmosphere right now. In my mind's eye I keep seeing a drunken woman strangling a man with some rope. He is sitting at a dining table desperately trying to loosen the ligature . . . and there is a plate of stew in front of him. (Why am I getting THAT information!) But he doesn't pass over at that moment and I'm sure he survived her attack and lived for many years afterwards with her. This is ridiculous but I feel they really loved each other! When they were drunk they were crazy and fought like cat and dog. Nothing else to report I'm afraid . . . need more answers.

2.13 a.m.

Still in rear garden. This is mad! I thought my eyes were playing tricks until a few moments ago. The male spirit, a female spirit and the two children are all staring at me in

silence from about thirty feet away at the rear wall. I am
going to walk towards them and find out what they want
and why all this supernatural phenomena is going on.
Here goes, I'm walking now . . .

2.23 a.m.
In lower hall. Shone my torch on the group of spirits
earlier and they vanished . . . I just know they still think
this is their home and are very upset at these flats being
built here. I can hear someone moving about upstairs
again but won't waste my time by going up. Sick of the
silly games spirit play – sick of spirit! Want to go home
now.

2.32 a.m.
Still in lower hall. Have attempted to spiritually cleanse
the entire place over the last few minutes and have been
hit square on the nose with a nail! As I sit here I have
summoned the spirits . . . I can see them all walking slowly
towards me . . . they are now encircling me and I'm feeling
very nervous!

I then asked the spirits why they were there and the male
became extremely angry and called me a 'trespasser' I
asked again and was psychically shown their respective
deaths in the house that once stood there: the two
children had died young and the poor parents had lived
the rest of their physical lives in mourning and had no
more children. As far as I could decipher, nothing
suspicious had happened and they simply felt bound to
the grounds of their house many years after their physical
deaths.

As I began to pray and ask them to move on, the most chilling experience of the evening occurred – I began to feel the sensation of something being placed around my neck and of being strangled! After a few moments of intense choking I fell to the ground and stared up to see the female spirit who was standing above me . . . she had a strange smile on her face, yet I felt she was definitely warning me to go. I could take the hint so pulled myself up and decided there and then to leave this horrible location and its ghostly owners behind. I'd been hit with a nail that had narrowly missed my eyes and now I was being choked by unseen hands. This was no 'normal' haunting – this was dangerous poltergeist activity and I had reached the conclusion that I could do nothing to prevent it.

As I made my way off the site I turned to see several shadows watching me. I then proceeded to give them all a real piece of my mind (can't print the words here I'm afraid) and finished by telling them how unfair they were being to the young families that were moving in and that life goes on. I must have looked like a real madman to any passers by as I stood shouting angrily at thin air, but I knew the spirit family were listening and in my fury I couldn't have cared less who else was around. In my last notes it's quite obvious in hindsight that I was tired, angry and a wee bit confused.

3.09 a.m.
Sitting outside site now in the fresh morning air – can do no more. Nearly blinded by a nail earlier and then choked half to death! (A bit of an exaggeration!) No more of this . . . no more investigations . . . no more readings and no more contact with spirits – unless they're bottled.

101

Every time I look back I'm sure I can see them watching me from within . . . I pity the poor people who choose to live in this paranormal dump in the future . . . I need a drink!

A while later John arrived and drove me back home. I hardly said a word all the way back.

However, John phoned me a few months later to tell me that all the ghosts seemed to have left – he was delighted. I revisited the site with him again and much to my surprise the place now seemed very peaceful and there had been no more poltergeist activity reported by anybody in the location. By that time most of the flats were occupied, the freshly planted flowerbeds were beginning to bloom and thankfully none of the wealthy residents there knew about the strange events that had taken place earlier that year.

After a tour of the building, which looked splendid in the daylight, we walked down the stairway towards the main door. I felt happy and contented but I had one of those strange feelings that something was watching us from behind and as I turned around I'm sure I briefly saw a little spirit figure standing on the top floor staring down at us – I was thankful that John seemed blissfully unaware of it though.

As we drove away that afternoon I was glad there had been no more activity in the building but I must say I'm convinced that the spirit family are still there, moving quietly through the shadows of the building, trying not to be noticed by residents. Who knows, maybe my rant as I left the premises that night stopped the activity. Or could it be that they are now quite content to exist side by side with the living? Or as many sceptics would argue, was it all some mass hallucination and the spirit family were simply figments of our imagination?

I guess you, the reader, will come up with your own conclusions but even as I write it here I can still feel a chill run down my spine when I think of the family who never left their home.

6

GHOSTS OF LEISURE

The lights, the smell of the greasepaint, the laughter, the tears and the applause – it is every performer's dream to gain hard-earned recognition for their talent on the stage, and when they've made it into the limelight some of them simply refuse to leave . . . even after death. I've personally had a couple of brushes with thespian ghosts and so, it seems, have many others.

Theatres were once the only entertainment available for the masses, and Scotland has had many illustrious buildings that have resonated with all kinds of emotions within their walls. Audiences from a bygone age would have walked in from the smoke-filled, dark-grey streets outside, trying to leave the cares and worries of their lives behind as they demanded to be entertained by the performers, both local and international, who risked their all by playing to the notoriously difficult Scottish mob.

Probably the most infamous theatre of them all in the twentieth century was the Glasgow Empire. It is said that the audiences were so merciless the place was unofficially called the 'Graveyard for English Comics'. Many comedians who later became TV stars suffered the deadly silence or the boos, hisses and abusive banter of the drunken Friday-night house and lived to tell the tale. There's one story I heard about Mike and Bernie Winters, two brothers who became huge television stars in the '70s.

They played the Empire early on in their careers. Their act began with Mike Winters onstage himself for a while until his brother, Bernie, would finally peek his face through the curtain and get laughs . . . usually! As Bernie's face appeared on cue at the Empire, a wee Glesga voice shouted from the silence 'Aw naw, there's two of them!' No doubt hundreds of performers 'died' this way on the Empire and other similar stages throughout Scotland, but for every tear of sadness shed there have also been tears of laughter, joy and appreciation.

If the 'stone tape' theory (where memories and emotions are imprinted onto the fabric of a building or place and replayed later) is true then just imagine the number of 'recordings' there are in any theatre! Firstly, there are the numerous audience members over the years that have been emotionally influenced by the happy or sad events onstage and off. Then, let's not forget the performers, both on and behind the scenes that undoubtedly will have been filled with nervousness, anxiety and excitement before a show and exhilaration or humiliation and disappointment afterwards. All of this creative psychic energy, mixed with the superstitions and egos of the theatrical world makes our dramatic locations the perfect scenes for hauntings and ghosts.

In every town or city there are also numerous pubs and hotels that claim to have an extra spirit or two behind the bar and if you think about it, they are also an ideal place for activity to occur due to the usually large turnover of people who have walked through the doors every day.

I've been invited to numerous drinking establishments throughout Scotland to come and investigate the strange goings on that the owners and staff claim to experience in their workplace. When I arrive I usually find out that the 'haunting' is nothing more than the product of the staff members' overactive imaginations and tall tales passed on through time by inebriated customers but occasionally there is some truth behind the stories.

If you think about it, old pubs, just like theatres, will have had a whole array of emotions felt and displayed within them, fuelled by booze. Punters may have relaxed after a hard day's graft or drowned their sorrows, had a laugh, spoken about the fitba', argued and fought with other punters and left the place to face the reality of real life at the end of the night.

Could the 'stone tape' theory mentioned above possibly be happening with pub hauntings too? But then again, not all pubs that have reported paranormal activity are old. One thing is for sure though: many pubs and theatres do seem to have strange goings-on that baffle the people there.

Whether there is any validity to this is a matter of personal opinion of course, but I firmly believe that certain events *can* leave a residual stain on the atmosphere of a location and pubs, hotels and inns would be obvious places for this kind of activity. However, a few pubs I've visited have definite spiritual presences that do seem to interact with customers and staff alike and it does seem these entities haven't listened when last orders were called.

Here are some interesting theatres, nearby public houses and places where it's said that ghosts have been seen. You will notice that I haven't included the *names* of the pubs. I did this because I had no intention of listing them all – I've only included the ones I've personally visited because of the possibility of leaving other allegedly haunted boozers out. So this will be your first test of psychic intuition . . . *you* can become a ghost detective and find the haunted pubs!

OK, I'll begin with a Glasgow theatre. The Tron Theatre, situated in the Trongate area of the city is very haunted I'm told. The steeple part of the building is all that remains from the original sixteenth-century edifice because the rest of the building was razed to the ground in 1793 after the 'Hellfire Club' – a bunch of drunken yobs – burned the place to the ground. The rest was soon rebuilt again and the exterior of the building remains very similar to the way it looked all those years ago.

Nowadays, the theatre is home to some great dramatic performances and the restaurant and bar serve excellent food and drink but there have been many paranormal experiences reported by staff and patrons over the years. These include figures seen wearing fashions of a long-gone age and a menacing presence felt in the boiler-room area as well as activity and apparitions in the auditorium itself. I haven't felt any distinct presences during my (too) frequent visits to the bar, but have sensed some strong residual energies. I haven't had access to the areas where the entities allegedly manifest.

It definitely is a nice place to visit though, have a drink and enjoy some great performances – and possibly see a 'cast member' who isn't supposed to be there.

Just a short walk through the Cross, along from the Tron Theatre in the Gallowgate area, next to the Barras Market, is a wonderful wee pub that is filled with great characters and the occasional spook too! The place is an institution in Glasgow and should be on any ghost hunter's 'to do' list. I've done a paranormal investigation there before and can categorically state that the place is an amazing location to sense spirit *and* enjoy a beer or spirit (of the other kind) in a down to earth Glasgow establishment that has stood for many years. The place is built on the site of an original inn which went back hundreds of years and it seems that some of the old customers and staff who once frequented the pub from bygone years have chosen to hang around. The hospitality is great and the spirit contact I personally received was phenomenal. Well worth a visit . . . if you can find it. If you walk up the High Street, from Glasgow Cross, there are several pubs in the area that claim to be haunted and I do agree, so it is worth popping in . . . just for research of course!

As you stroll up the High Street, notice the wall on your right. This is part of the wall where Duke Street Prison was once situated. Many people were hanged in the prison and if you look closely there are bullet holes on the wall from a shootout that occurred in 1921 when gunmen fired on a prison van as they attempted to free a dangerous prisoner. Continue up the High Street and you will see Provand's Lordship, otherwise known as the Oldest House in Glasgow. The house was originally built in 1471 as part of St Nicholas's Hospital by the Bishop of Glasgow. Step inside and feel the residual energies of many generations of Glaswegians and you might even be lucky enough to be transported in your mind back through time.

Just across the road is Glasgow Cathedral, one of my own favourite spiritual places in Scotland. This building was consecrated in 1197 and is one of the greatest examples of religious architecture anywhere. To sit in the pews in the quietude and admire the surroundings is a hugely uplifting experience.

Just next to the cathedral is the Necropolis. This Victorian 'City of the Dead' is an amazing place where the grand monuments are a testament to Glasgow's long-dead wealthy citizens and architects. The place is worth a visit for anyone but if you have some psychic intuition and show respect, you may experience some phenomena. I did when I was a naïve young man, as I've mentioned earlier in the book. So, onward we go.

Another theatre that is reputedly haunted is the Village Theatre, East Kilbride. It's been said that a former worker who died many years ago has been seen backstage a few times since. I was told about him by staff members when I did a psychic floorshow there in 2006 but can honestly say I didn't see any apparitions or sense anything strange or paranormal backstage. Something odd did happen, though, as we were leaving at the end of the night long after the show had finished. I had a strong feeling we were being watched from within as we exited the quiet, empty building and when I turned I saw a shadow moving from behind the outside door – but we were ninety-nine per cent sure no one was there. The overall feeling of the place was warm and welcoming and great for a show.

The nearby old town area of East Kilbride is a great place to wander through and is filled with residual history but I haven't seen much paranormal activity during my visits.

Some ghosts and manifestations seem to prefer to remain hidden in the shadows of theatres. One such spirit has been seen lurking in the plush surroundings of the

Edinburgh Festival Theatre; he is reported to be a tall, dark figure and is said to have been a member of an illusion act called 'The Great Lafayette' who was tragically killed by a disastrous fire in the early twentieth century. There has been a theatre on the site since 1830 but the present theatre which was built later has been used as many things, including a bingo hall. (If you've ever seen a bingo game in full swing you'd see *real* emotions – a definite candidate for later hauntings by aggrieved grannies!) A former employee of the theatre told me that she got so used to the presence of the 'magician ghost' being around that she stopped being frightened and used to quietly say 'hi' to him when she sensed or saw him.

Staying in Edinburgh, a pal of mine who is an actor told me about an experience he once had while working at the Edinburgh Playhouse. He had heard stories of haunted theatres many times before and had never really seen or sensed anything paranormal before, but one afternoon as the dress-rehearsal for the show he was performing in was going on, from the stage he could see a shadowy figure moving from the back of the stalls and standing at the left-hand aisle for a few moments. He originally thought it was someone connected to the cast until the figure vanished in front of his eyes. There have been other sightings reported of an apparition in a grey coat and cold spots throughout the area when the ghost is around.

It's said that Edinburgh is the most haunted city in Europe, so it would obviously have some haunted theatres and pubs within its boundaries, and I have to agree; not too far from the Playhouse is Rose Street, with lots of pubs, some allegedly haunted by ghosts and some haunted by stag parties. But further up the hill is the oldest part of the city which has numerous alleged haunted boozers.

The old town area of Edinburgh is packed with pubs, many of which are said to be haunted. I've spent many an evening visiting the drinking establishments in the area (it's a hard job but someone has to do it) and can testify that many of them are indeed very haunted.

I decided not to name them for fear of forgetting other ones but I'd advise any avid ghost hunter, psychic or historian to visit as many establishments in the old town and Grassmarket as they can. For anyone sitting at the tables outside the pubs in the Grassmarket enjoying a light refreshment on a summer's night, it's very easy to forget you're only yards away from the exact spot where the gallows once stood and many guilty – and innocent – people saw their last moments of their physical lives.

It's always worth visiting Greyfriar's Cemetery: this is where the 'Greyfriar's Bobby' story unfolded. More about that later though.

This cemetery is alleged to be one of the most haunted locations in the world and is the site of the famous Mackenzie Poltergeist. It is said the spirit of George Mackenzie, a man who it is documented took delight in persecuting covenanters (people who refused to accept the king as head of the Church, and many of whom were imprisoned here for their beliefs) still haunts the grounds, scratching, pushing and hitting visitors who dare to walk near the tombs of his victims. It is said the phenomena began after Mackenzie's tomb was disturbed a few years back. I've been there lots of times and haven't come in contact with Mackenzie personally but have seen many apparitions of young men and women haunting the grounds of this fine cemetery. It is quite a disturbing place though and I'd advise anyone to be cautious and protected.

Just like the alleged spirit present in the Village Theatre, earlier, His Majesty's Theatre in Aberdeen is said to have a resident ghost who wasn't a performer either. It is said that a man who worked as a stage hand was sadly killed in the mid-twentieth century and present-day phenomena such as moving objects, strange noises and dark apparitions backstage are attributed to him. The entire theatre, which was built in 1906 and was recently refurbished, is a magnificent place to eat, drink and enjoy some great theatrical performances. I watched a show there recently and definitely picked up some very strong residual energy in this wonderful place but sadly didn't see the ghost.

However, walk along to St Nicholas Church in the heart of Aberdeen and walk through the beautiful graveyard and you may see the alleged spirit of a young lady dressed in white who some have witnessed in the past. I sadly didn't see her the day I was there, but there was an amazing sense of a presence following us about. It could have been my imagination though.

In the mid '90s I was alone in the Pearce Institute Theatre, in Govan, after watching some of my friends rehearsing a play. When they left for lunch I sat on the front row of seats and read a newspaper waiting for them to return. After a few minutes I began to get an eerie feeling I was being watched from behind but put it down to imagination. After another few minutes there was a faint smell of pipe tobacco and I just knew something was behind me – as I turned around a clear figure of an old man was seated in a chair a few rows back, staring blankly at the stage. He was white headed and quietly puffing away on a pipe. He wore glasses and seemed very well dressed as if he may have been dressed for an occasion. After a few moments he turned his head, looked directly at me and evaporated into thin air and that was the only time I saw him throughout my frequent visits there. I never found out who he was or why he appeared in the theatre beside me that afternoon but I must say, he definitely seemed very at home and relaxed in the fourth row.

Well, when it comes to Govan and Kinning Park, I have to say I'm a wee bit biased! A little pub directly across the road from the Pearce Institute is a definite favourite of mine; good beer and banter. I haven't heard any stories about the place being haunted but the surrounding area outside is full of ghosts. So this friendly pub is a great stop-off before or after visiting the awesome Govan Old Parish Church Graveyard (which I write about earlier in the book). Further along towards the city centre is Paisley Road Toll. There are a few old fashioned bars here that I can say are well worth visiting.

If you travel to Scotland Street School, which is now a museum of education, there are definitely many energies present in this building.

This school (also my late mother's school) was designed by Charles Rennie Mackintosh between 1903 and 1906. You see classroom reconstructions and really get a sense of the history of Scottish education. Although it isn't reported to be haunted, I sensed a definite form of an old-fashioned female teacher in a corridor which faded after a few moments – a great place to go and visit.

Heading back to Auld Reekie (Edinburgh) and theatres, the Royal Lyceum theatre is said to be haunted by a spirit who allegedly appears high above the stage on the lighting rig. Some say it seems to be a female figure. I spoke to someone a while back who worked there many years ago and he told me that although he hadn't personally seen anything paranormal, some of the actors and staff members he worked with through the years had witnessed some strange goings on that couldn't simply be put down to imagination.

The theatre, which was built in 1883, has seen some great performances as the greatest actors and actresses of the Victorian age trod the boards of this fine building in its early years. Nowadays, the productions range from the classics to modern dramas and as I sat there one night a while back, I could imagine the actors from bygone times delivering some of those very same lines that were being performed many years later on the same stage. I was struck by its brilliant interior and love the place but I didn't personally sense or witness any phenomena that evening as an audience member, only some residual feelings.

One thing's for sure though, the Royal Lyceum is a great venue to sit back and be entertained in and has excellent historical surroundings which resound with many vibes from the past.

Back in Glasgow, I have to say my favourite theatre in the whole of Scotland is the Pavilion Theatre. I've sat through many great shows in this place and even performed (badly) in one a long time ago. The theatre was built in 1904 and has seen very little alteration since then, so it really is a case of stepping back in time as you enter the doors of this Glasgow institution. All types of great performers have played here, from the great Harry Lauder, Tommy Morgan, Lex McLean and a very young Charlie Chaplin to modern-day stars like Billy Connolly and Lulu. It's one of the only privately run theatres in the UK and receives no money from the authorities, so it is completely independent.

Two experiences I had while I was a chorus member of a show in 1994 gave me the chills at the time. I was standing in the lower corridor of the dressing-rooms waiting to go on stage when a pretty young girl walked past me wearing a bright blue dress and a tiara. She smiled at me as I stepped aside and let her pass. I then quickly glanced the other way and when I turned back she had gone. There was really nowhere she could have gone to as the cast and crew were the only people in the whole building to my knowledge. I didn't see her again and no one I asked had seen anyone passing by them. Even to this day I can remember the scent of her strong perfume as clear as if it was yesterday. I've since heard rumours that a young dancer was killed in the theatre many years ago in the top dressing-rooms. If this is true, could it have been the same girl? Whoever it was she seemed to be content and interacted with me.

I did hear at the time that the ghost of the great Tommy Morgan haunted the theatre after his ashes were spread on the roof when he died but I had felt nothing (except pre-show nerves) for the first few days of the play's run. However, one afternoon I was sitting on stage an hour or so before the last show. As I sat drinking some water I glanced up at the box-seats on the right and saw a large man leaning over and grinning down at me. The image only lasted a split second to be honest, so the possibility of it being a trick of the light or imagination is strong I suppose. I have to admit it wasn't until a good few years later that I saw a photograph of Tommy Morgan and he was the spitting image of the figure I had briefly seen in the box that afternoon. If the Glasgow Pavilion theatre is indeed haunted by the stars of yesteryear then it seems the apparitions I witnessed are extremely happy to be there and I can understand why.

There are other reputedly haunted theatres in the country that I haven't touched on or visited yet, for instance the Britannia Panopticon Music Hall, which is a stone's throw from the aforementioned Tron Theatre in Glasgow's Trongate area. The theatre is in disuse these days but is a great hidden piece of Scotland's theatrical history and has many tales of paranormal phenomena that would be a great visit for any avid ghost hunter or historian. So let's hope it can be refurbished one day in the future.

Just around the corner on Stockwell Street is an old Glasgow watering hole that is allegedly haunted too. It's one of those pubs where you sit down and don't want to leave . . . maybe that's why it's haunted.

Someone emailed me a while back telling me the modern-built Eden Court Theatre, in their home town of Inverness, is allegedly haunted by a woman and a little child who walk the grounds. And someone else told me that a strangely dressed old man appeared outside the place one night, asked them what time it was and as they looked back up he had disappeared!

Sometimes it seems that building work causes some kind of paranormal activity (as I have written about in an earlier chapter) so the old ghosts and the newly-built theatre in question are totally unrelated in that instance. The Theatre Royal, Glasgow, is another great building that is allegedly haunted by a girl who failed an audition many years ago and committed suicide as a result of her failure.

Whether the stories of tragedy and happiness that cause our country's many houses of entertainment and drinking-dens to be haunted by the dead are fact or fiction doesn't really matter. Every building or area has a story attached to it – the story of the people who built it, inhabited the place and worked in it, and we are simply another chapter in that story. So if one person from the many thousands who lived and breathed in a location at some time in their physical lives decided to *either come back and visit* or *stay on* a wee while longer, then what place would attract a spirit to remain 'earthbound' more than one of our great theatres or a much-loved pub? There's an old saying, 'If these walls could talk.' Well, in the emotional, historic and dramatic world of Scottish theatre and pubs, maybe they do.

There are many other pubs throughout Scotland that are allegedly haunted. For instance, travel to Larkhall and visit one of the country's most haunted inns that serves good food and beer. Or travel down the road to Lanark and enjoy the banter in a fantastic old hotel that has seen apparitions of monks. So, you don't have to sit in the darkness in the middle of the night at a haunted location to experience the paranormal first-hand. All you have to do is sit back, relax and keep your ears and eyes open in one of our many haunted pubs and inns. It does seem that more paranormal activity happens in a relaxed atmosphere, so where better than places of leisure? I realise I've probably missed out many places here, but someday I might get round to visiting them all and telling you about them. It's a hard job but somebody's got to do it!

7

PSYCHIC ANIMALS, GHOSTLY
BATTLES AND BEASTIES

I must say that being a psychic has put me in touch with many weird and wonderful people, most of whom I'm glad to have met, but very occasionally I've been approached by some strange sorts who claim to have extraordinary powers and are bordering on lunacy.

One such person (who shall remain nameless) came to me for a reading in 1999 and proceeded to tell me they were the world's greatest psychic and the reincarnation of Genghis Kahn, Jack the Ripper and Mozart! A mad Mongol leader, a serial killer and musical genius all rolled into one and alone in a room with yours truly. It's moments like that when I wish I had a normal job!

Thankfully, most people I've met who are involved in the esoteric world are kind, well-meaning individuals who are simply following their life path and hoping to help people along the way. Of course there will be charlatans and con artists but sadly every line of business has people like that. The real task is to find the genuine people out there and try to weed out the fraudsters who take people's money and prey on the vulnerability of grief, heartache and desperation.

When people mention the word 'psychic' most people think of someone with tarot cards, a crystal ball or some other divination tool performing a reading, or a medium on a stage giving messages from beyond the grave, but the whole psychic world has many varied practitioners out there, all of whom believe wholeheartedly in their different abilities.

One area that I've been very interested in over the past few years is 'Animal Communication'. This is where a practitioner can allegedly communicate directly with an animal and sense its feelings and thoughts and even pick up symptoms of any illness from them. This was an ability I thought was a wee bit daft until I saw it performed first-hand and must say I was really impressed.

Animals can be a great comfort to us through our physical existence and the unconditional love they bestow upon their human friends can be phenomenal. Many people's lives have been saved by animals throughout history and the acts of loyalty that have been written about and documented are incredible. Take, for instance, the Edinburgh tale of 'Greyfriars Bobby'. Most people know the story which centres around a wee dog who spent fourteen years standing over his master, policeman John Gray's, grave after he died in 1858. The only time it's said Bobby would leave the grave is when the one o'clock gun was fired and he'd run for his dinner, stuff his wee face then return to the grave again! There have been several films made and books written about the subject and if you walk through Edinburgh, there is a monument and pub named after Bobby. If you visit the Museum of Edinburgh on the Canongate, you can see some really interesting artefacts; among other things, Bobby's feeding bowl and collar. As well as being an interesting tale of love and loyalty, the residual psychic energy from the wee dog's belongings is very strong. Well worth a visit! I personally believe the wee dog could probably see his John's spirit and that's why he remained there for so long but that's just my opinion.

Animals have played a part in the lives and superstitions of Scottish people for many years and have been believed to have brought good luck, bad luck or even to have cured all sorts of disease and illnesses.

In old times roast mouse was said to be a cure for whooping cough and a howling dog outside the house was seen as a very bad omen indeed; it allegedly foretold the death of one of the inhabitants.

It seems our ancient ancestors feared our canine friends on occasion too because a creature called 'Black Angus' or 'Fairy Dog' was a huge dangerous black hound that it was said roamed the Scottish countryside and was rather noticeable because of its yellow eyes and large teeth. At least all we have to worry about in modern Scotland is midges!

I, like many others, have enjoyed the comfort and friendship that a wee animal can give a human. They do seem to have a built-in sixth sense and the numerous strange tales that people have told me about their pets over the years has convinced me that most of our furry – and feathered – friends have some kind of heightened sensitivity.

I have to admit I become angry when I hear some people say animals have no soul – I'd say the people who spout nonsense like that have no brain more like! Of course they have a soul.

Many times in the past an animal has come through to someone in a sitting I've given. Of course the pet can't actually *talk* to me but the accurate description and undying love that are there can give great comfort to someone who has lost a beloved animal.

That reminds me of one sitting I did a few years back when an old man walked in the room and sat down in front of me. An old dog walked in beside him and lay beside his feet and at first I have to admit I didn't realise the old creature was in spirit. It was only after a few minutes when the man informed me that he'd lost his old four-legged pal a month before that I realised the dog was in the spirit realm! He was a big hairy dog who was obviously dedicated and loyal to his old human friend, even after the death of his physical being. Needless to say, the old man was very emotional and comforted when I described his late companion who remained with him. The old man left the room that day contented that his old pal had no intention of leaving his earthly pal's side as they left together.

Something similar happened to me when I was eighteen years old. My wee mongrel dog, Laddie, who we'd had for eleven years and was such a great part of the family, died and I was deeply heartbroken. But every night like clockwork, I'd hear his wee spirit entering my room and feel him jump onto the bottom of the bed and lie down at my feet – just the way he'd done for most of my life. This continued for some years until I moved away and he simply moved on in the spirit realm with a deceased family member.

Another strange story I experienced happened when I was wee and the whole area in Possilpark in Glasgow where we lived was being renovated. We had a great dog called Major, so when the renovations began my mother decided that Major should be taken to my uncle's house because of the upset the constant hammering and drilling of the workmen were causing him.

We took him on the bus one evening and travelled some miles across the whole length of the city, from north to south, to where my uncle lived. The dog seemed very happy to be there so we left my uncle's house feeling a bit emotional but sure that the dog would have a pleasant time. We then got back on the bus and travelled the many miles back home. It must have been about 1 a.m. when the constant barking outside roused us. When we went to the window, there was Major, soaked through with his paws bleeding! He had bolted from my uncle's and had run all the way to the other side of Glasgow, back to our house. Now, I completely disregard any sceptical argument in this case and the only possibility is that the dog had some kind of sixth sense and instinct that led him through strange streets and dark fields all the way back to us that night. Remember, he had been taken on a bus and had *never* walked the route in his life – mainly because it was too far. Incidentally, my uncle's house was by far the most haunted place I've ever seen. I've heard many similar cases where animals manage to somehow find a way home against all odds and I'm fascinated by every story.

The evidence I've heard and experienced completely convinces me that the wee souls of animals do live on and they do try and communicate in their own way – but what about animals communicating with us in this life?

Well, I have to admit that I've never experienced any direct psychic communication from a living animal but as I said already I have seen some compelling evidence that there is possibly some kind of telepathic connection between animal communicators and pets.

For instance, one time an animal communicator walked into our house, took a look at the pet cats we had and instantly told us all about our cats' personalities. All of the info she picked up was true and there was absolutely no way she could have known any of this in advance – I was impressed. She then proceeded to give us a running commentary on all our pets and I have to admit, some of the information was spot on!

It seems strange, and even a bit odd, to hear someone talking on your cats' behalf and I'd never have believed it before that day. I guess I can't mock though because I talk to the dead. At least my cats didn't have anything too bad to say about me!

Animal communicators claim to be able to help with the emotional and physical problems of a pet too and some even claim to be able to communicate with them telepathically after death. When I see an animal in spirit they are exactly as they were on this side of life but at no stage do I receive words, pictures or messages from them. Some animal psychics say the animals can actually *talk* to them – wouldn't that be an amazing gift to have.

Lorraine Kenyon is a pal of mine and an animal communicator who is based in Lanarkshire. She runs great workshops and really has an affinity with dogs, cats and all sorts of animals. I asked Lorraine exactly how animals communicate with her when she meets them – do they use words and sentences? Lorraine tells me, 'They (animals) do use words when communicating and give the names of the people they share their lives with or have done in the past. The information can come in many forms – I have even heard songs that have been significant to the animals' guardians from them.

They also give information to me through pictures and feelings and when they've passed into spirit, the information from them actually flows more quickly.'

So, animals take in a lot more of their surroundings than we give them credit for. They know more about us than we think they do and it seems they do communicate freely after their physical deaths. They have emotions, sensitivity and, according to Lorraine, a definite understanding of the past and the present. In fact she says there have been times when animals have actually made predictions for their human friends! A female chinchilla Lorraine worked with once, foretold that her guardian would have trouble with her ovaries and a few months later it happened. Was it just a strange coincidence? I personally don't think so and believe that when a bond of love exists between any beings, a deep psychic connection occurs and when an animal loves its guardian unconditionally, the connection may be even stronger.

Lorraine tells me there are many amazing experiences of animal precognition and communication that inspire her to continue her great work helping animals to have a voice.

Maybe we, who call ourselves their 'masters', have much to learn from them. So, next time someone calls them 'dumb' animals, they may be the 'dumb' ones and there is a whole lot more to those wee beings who have the tough job of sharing their world with a cruel and destructive species . . . us.

Another communicator I met a while back seems to have a real affinity with horses in particular and is now snowed under with requests from owners and riders who are desperate to know what their horses are thinking about and are seeking help for the happiness and health of their animals.

A young girl had emailed me to say that her horse was becoming extremely agitated and seemed frightened to leave the stables in the morning. She asked if I could help in some way by visiting and 'reading' the horse. I knew I'd have been well out of my depth with a case like that (and didn't fancy a hoof in the stomach) so I gave her the number of a few animal psychics to call, including the woman above who specialises in horses. It must have been a week or two later when the owner emailed me back and told me that the lady who came out to visit was able to tell her that the horse had once cut its back left leg in the field and was scared in case it happened again. The communicator advised her to cover the horse's leg and move an old rusty wheelbarrow that lay in the field. When she did this the horse looked as happy as . . . well, as happy as a horse can look (I won't do the silly gag about 'why the long face?') and now he walks around the field freely.

But it just goes to show that there has to be a psychic connection going on between communicator and animal which can be extremely beneficial for the welfare and health of our animal friends. And to witness a genuine animal communicator like Lorraine in action is a sight to behold.

At the time of writing, there are many courses out there that claim to teach animal communication – and just like the many 'psychic development' courses that fill the internet, I'd be wary and check out the credentials, history and feedback of the teachers before parting with your cash. I've tried many times myself to communicate with animals psychically but nothing evidential has come to me and the animals involved have soon grown tired of my feeble attempts. So, I'll stick to human spirits I think and leave animal communication to the people who seem to have the gift.

If, as I believe, the spirits of animals do survive physical death, then maybe their ghosts haunt us the way human entities do? Well, if we were to look at the many sightings of ghosts and apparitions throughout the country, we can see that ghostly animals do make an appearance now and again.

One story was relayed to me when I was young and used to drive motorbikes with my mates up to the village of Fintry. We ended up getting to know the locals while having a wee drink in the local establishment. It was there that some customers told me about the ghosts of the local Culcreuch Castle: a grey man, a lady and a ghostly piper have been seen. However, I am fascinated by the reports that one of the ghosts was a floating animal head allegedly seen around the ramparts.

A long time ago, Ballechin House in Tayside was also the scene of some strange goings on after the owner swore to return after death in the body of one of his dogs. The place showed all the signs of being haunted after his dogs died too. For instance, the smell of dogs stank the house out, there were rappings on the wall, an apparition of a dog appeared frequently, the apparent fluttering of the wings of an invisible bird could be heard and felt and the sound of a large animal throwing itself against the doors (and people's legs) could be heard. This, accompanied by thuds, moans and icy chills stirred the interest of some Victorian paranormal investigators who stayed at the house after a family deserted the place in terror. The investigators also claimed to have experienced some strange phenomena too while they were there. During a communication board session, they came in contact with a female spirit who it's said asked them to visit the nearby glen at sunset. When they arrived at the glen they saw the figure of a nun moving through the snow who then vanished in front of their eyes as she reached a tree. The same figure was allegedly seen several times afterwards by different onlookers. Sadly the place was demolished in the early 1960s but the surrounding area is still worth a visit.

One of Edinburgh's – and Scotland's – alleged most haunted locations is the famous Mary King's Close in the old town area of the city. This is another location where ghostly animals have also been witnessed on occasion and is one of my favourite places. This underground street lay forgotten for many years but now the place has been opened up to the public and has been the subject of many investigations and visiting psychics over the last few years. It is a wonderful dark, cavernous location where the visitor's mind can't fail to picture the scene and the people who once lived in the cramped tenement houses so long ago. Some of the inhabitants of the street sadly fell victim to the plague in the 1600s and many present-day visitors have sworn to have experienced the ghostly victims of the past haunting the place. For instance, a wee girl called 'Annie' was sensed by a visiting Japanese psychic in the early 1990s and now her room is filled with toys from people who have been on the tour. There have been many apparitions here and strangely, many of the visions of animals that have been seen in the close were reported to have been headless.

Some people claim that some of the ghosts of dogs that have been sighted throughout Scotland are actually people who return and choose to show themselves as animals. I have absolutely no idea why a human being in the spirit world would wish to do such a thing but some people still believe this to be true . . . some even say that demons show themselves in this way too. For instance, there are some places throughout the country that have similar stories to Inchdrewer Castle in Aberdeen, where reports of a ghostly white dog that haunts the area is said to be the spirit of a lady who prefers to appear in that form.

Staying in the area for a moment, a place I visited a while back is Slains Castle, which, although in ruins, is an amazing place for spiritual contact and psychic energy. It is said that the castle was the inspiration behind Bram Stoker's novel *Dracula*. Bram had stayed in a nearby hotel while writing the novel and was so inspired by the scene that it's said he set his novel there but altered it at a later date.

Standing in the ruins of the castle, it isn't hard to understand why a writer could be inspired by such a place because the views are spectacular and the sense of history is incredible.

There have also been sightings here of many apparitions, including marching soldiers from World War II. A ghostly old horse and carriage has been seen several times too.

I went there and received definite spiritual contact from a young girl from the seventeenth century and two men from the Victorian era and the connection I had with them all was fantastic and I really left the place uplifted! I'd say this is one of Scotland's psychic – and historical – gems and anyone interested in residual history, meditating and psychic development should visit this place at least once. But be careful of the nearby cliffs and bunkers – they're very dangerous.

It seems strange that there are so many sightings of ghostly riders on horseback or of horses pulling carriages – if these are genuine phenomena and not just some form of hallucinations then, could the rider and horses still exist side by side in the spirit realm as they did in this life?

Some sightings of carriages are even more detailed. JT from Motherwell emailed me with a story:

Hi Tom,

I was waiting for a lift to work one morning about 5.30 a.m. in 1993 at Crossgates in Bellshill (I start at 6.00 a.m.) when I heard the sound of horses' hoofs. For a few moments I stood trying to find out where the sound was coming from but couldn't pinpoint it. Suddenly a large coach driven by two horses appeared from around the corner and was heading towards my direction.

For about twenty seconds I could see all of the details of the horses, and the driver, who had a small round hat on. I thought to myself it must have been some fancy dress gimmick until it vanished in front of my eyes.

I swear I wasn't drinking and felt completely wide awake but I needed a drink after, believe me Tom. I am dumbfounded as to why I seen (sic) it that dark morning and I've never seen it before or since in all my years. Can you explain?

JT

Was JT seeing things? Did a lack of sleep cause him to hallucinate? Or did he really see an elaborate apparition of an old coach, complete with horses and driver? If this was a genuine paranormal experience, why would such a thing exist? I've never known any spirit being to 'need a lift' somewhere in a horse-drawn coach, or in any other vehicle for that matter so why would these ethereal beings show themselves like this? I don't have the answers sadly.

The fact is that many people have seen apparitions like this so the matter is definitely worth investigating further I'd say.

Although there were no animals involved, something along the same lines happened to a group of us many years ago but, thinking back, it could all have been the work of children's over-active imaginations and possibly some kind of mass hallucination – but I'll let you decide.

I must have been about nine or ten years old at the time when we paid a visit to my uncle's house in the Gorbals area of Glasgow. It was early evening when my older cousin and I and a couple of other local pals of hers decided to venture up to a disused railway track that runs through the area. We had heard all the stories of the local 'ghost train' and our wee hearts were filled with excitement as we climbed the embankment full of jaggy nettles and made our way onto the overgrown rusty old tracks. I vividly remember walking along the tracks when one of the group screamed 'there's the ghost train comin'!' We all began to run back to our point of entry, but when I turned round I swear there was this huge dark steam train making its way along the tracks towards us. I remember the whole scene as if it was yesterday; the smoke and the sound as the ghostly locomotive travelled along the broken tracks.

We ran back to my cousin's house that evening filled with excitement and fear as we relayed our story to our family.

It wasn't until recently that I was in contact with my cousin again and she said she remembered that day and remembered the 'ghost train' too.

Even as a psychic medium who has lived with the paranormal all his life, I find an experience like that bizarre. I totally understand spirit connection and life after death but must admit I'm baffled as to why a large train can appear in front of the eyes of children!

I personally think it was some kind of mass hysteria that overcame us that day but other people I've spoken to who have had similar experiences disagree and are convinced sightings like that are genuine apparitions, similar to visions of coaches drawn by horses who died long ago.

A similar apparition to my childhood experience, but obviously more tragic, has allegedly taken place numerous times at the scene of the Tay Bridge disaster. This horrific tragedy occurred on 28 December 1879 when a terrible storm and high winds caused the bridge to weaken and a train carrying over seventy passengers to plunge into the cold, dark waters below. No one knows exactly what technical problems caused the crash that night and there are a few theories as to why the bridge collapsed but the accident caused a major overhaul in the construction of bridges since. All of the passengers and crew sadly died at the scene and it's said that on the anniversary of that fateful night the screams of the poor victims can still be heard. Some people even claim to have seen a ghostly apparition of the train as it travels across the exact spot where the old bridge once stood, before re-enacting the fall to the icy grave below.

Quite by chance, I was at the place in 1999 on the anniversary of the tragedy and stood alone and quietly said a prayer for the souls of those who lost their lives all those years before. Thankfully, I didn't see or experience anything other than a distinct feeling of melancholy that night (which I'm sure wasn't paranormal) and I do hope the poor victims are now at peace with their loved ones.

It is strange to imagine something that is man-made to be seen or heard in the spirit world but many people have seen soldiers with guns and even heard the sound of cannons firing during the sighting of a battle apparition. It's very easy for someone of a sceptical nature to say that these sightings are all in the mind but what if they aren't? There is no proof that the witnesses of these phenomena *are* hallucinating and there is no proof that they aren't so for now I'll just take their word for it and deal with the facts at hand.

If the 'stone tape' theory exists then a scene of horror such as the Tay Bridge disaster must be stained with the residual emotions of those poor people meeting their deaths prematurely at the hands of fate. This could be why there have been sightings throughout the years on the anniversary, but when doing research for this book I noticed that the sightings now seem to have all but stopped. Why? Could this be because the *psychic stain* of such a horrific occurrence has slowly eroded through time or have we changed in some way? So what about battlefields? These sad areas seem to hold many emotions and Scotland's battles have been re-enacted many times in front of the eyes of numerous unlucky spectators.

Culloden is classed as one of the spookiest places in the country, where sights and sounds have been reported many times and many sights and sounds of the skirmish have been experienced. Now, if you don't know the history of Culloden then please go and buy a Scottish history book or look it up because I'm not telling ye all the details here!

It's said that on the anniversary of the battle, the sounds of soldiers fighting, steel clashing with steel and gunshots fill the air – and even the car park is said to be extremely haunted too.

I've visited the place many times and once I even managed to get there on the anniversary of the battle. I have to say I personally didn't see or hear anything unusual that day but the residual energy in the place is beyond belief and I had a splitting headache every time I walked to one particular area. I remember receiving communication from a fourteen-year-old soldier, but nothing too impressive. One client who came to me said she had just parked in the Culloden car park when she saw two young men dressed in old-fashioned clothes, walking horses on the field one morning; thinking this was a publicity stunt she opened her car and took out her camera – only to find the two boys and the horses had gone within a split second.

Just like battlefields all over the world where young men have lost their lives, I'd say the place is very active and it's nice to be respectful to any area where so many young souls left the physical world before their natural time.

I have to say that one of the most active locations (with the strangest names) I've come across in my life where I witnessed an apparition of an animal is situated in Lanarkshire, a few miles outside the town of Hamilton, on the road to Stonehouse. It's not a very well known place at all – its name is Plotcock Castle – and I'd advise most people of a psychic or sensitive disposition to stay away from the area.

A young witch who came to me for a reading many years back told me about the place and how she used to go there, perform her rituals and watch the ghosts of men and animals lurking in the woods.

I decided to visit the place one afternoon with Tom M and can say, in my opinion this is one of Scotland's most haunted locations. Psychically it is a very disturbing place and I wouldn't advise anyone to go there.

Plotcock Castle is no longer there and the area was, at the time, covered with trees and bushes so it was quite difficult to find at first but eventually her directions took us to the spot. As soon as we reached the location I saw what looked like a monk, kneeling and praying, and as the ghost lifted its head it vanished.

Now, here's the strangest and possibly most bizarre apparition I've seen in my life; a sinister-looking male figure stood in front of us holding a freshly decapitated goat's head and beside him was a huge fierce hound. He stared directly into my eyes for a moment, before holding up the severed head and walking towards us. Thankfully he faded away. Even the ever sceptical Tom M saw several 'shadows' and felt a real sense of foreboding in the place and wanted to leave. His words to me were, 'It really feels as if someone or something doesn't want us here and I think we shouldn't hang around.' The EMF detector he had was showing definite signs of activity and I saw visions of the dark arts being practised too for some reason. I then began to see visions of young men being brutally beaten and tortured which began to panic and disturb me a bit, and it was then I decided Tom M was right and we should leave. As we turned to walk away a small stone hit me on the back of the head (could have been wildlife I suppose) and when we left the area of Plotcock Castle behind, the residual screams of agony from so long ago still echoed in my head.

I've since been told that the place was once a prison in the dark distant past. Maybe this was the source of the visions of torture and the screams? I've never been back to find out though and have no intention of revisiting the site . . . ever!

Staying in the Lanarkshire area for a moment, another place which still rings with the residual stains of blood and fear is the scene of the battle of Bothwell Bridge. The battle took place in 1679 as the government tried to crush the covenanters, mentioned earlier in the book.

Nowadays, to stand in the field at the Bridge and witness the eerie silence around you is a strange feeling indeed and is well worth a visit for anyone interested in Scottish history. I believe many of the long-dead spirits of the battle still remain there and I have personally experienced some traumatic emotions during a vigil one night when I saw some soldiers running in terror.

So, it seems that animals do play as big a part in the afterlife as they do in the physical world. It looks likely they still stand by us, give us comfort and serve us even after death, but then again, as I've said before, they do have souls. But what about the sightings of old coaches, trains – and there are even reports of spirit cars, buses and planes – that have been seen by many people throughout the land? Does that mean the old saying 'you can't take it with you' is wrong? One thing's for sure; there will be many more sightings of ghostly animals and vehicles before we ever find the real answer . . . if we ever do.

So next time you are standing alone and waiting for a bus on a dark, cold night, check out the driver and make sure the vehicle is from this world.

8

GOODBYE AND HELLO AGAIN

For anyone interested in developing themselves and who feels they may have some hidden psychic or mediumistic abilities that are lying dormant within them waiting to blossom, always remember that people's lives and emotions should *never* be played with and any psychic or medium worth their salt should only give 100 per cent genuine information. Remember, a psychic is dealing with grief, heartache and vulnerability and must remain professional.

In this chapter I'll try to give some examples of the after-death communication I've experienced during private sittings and I'll also give some examples of the work of the unscrupulous who dwell on people's hopes and fears.

But first . . . it will happen to us all at least once in our physical lives; that feeling of emptiness, vulnerability, anger and deep sadness – a sadness that brings the delicate balance of our physical lives into perspective. This sadness makes us question aspects of this life and it clouds our view of the everyday world around us, making us feel alone and introverted. I'm speaking of 'grief', that horrible emotion that most living beings experience when they have lost a person who is so precious to them. For some, a psychic or medium can be their only hope of closure.

When this physical life ends and the new journey begins, it's very rare for people to return in spirit form and appear directly in front of their loved ones just to let them know they're OK, so the grieving family and friends are left to mourn the loss of that person. All that is left behind are the material possessions, photographs and memories of the precious time spent together in this, the physical world. But many people like me believe that the physical death is only the beginning of a long and wonderful journey of the soul and we will be reunited in time and can receive limited communication over lifetimes.

Throughout this book I've tended to concentrate on the spirits and ghosts who haunt this country and have written about the darker side of the psychic world I've come into contact with, but I have to say that nearly all of the spiritual contact I've ever received during sittings is uplifting and wonderful.

The contact usually begins when I receive some information about the characteristics of the spirit person trying to communicate that I'll pass on to the person in front of me for validation. Sometimes I'm given their name, their job and little details that would seem unimportant to anyone else but mean a lot to both people in either worlds who are trying to reach out.

I can often *see* the actual spirit person manifest in front of my eyes and have to say this is one of the most amazing and emotional sights imaginable and even after so many years, it never fails to move me. Many times the spirit person will stroke the hair of their loved one here, or kiss them gently on the head. The person on this side of life can often feel the icy sensation (or warmth) generated in the area their deceased loved one is touching at that moment. It really is a wonderful picture when someone who maybe passed away some years before comes through and spiritually embraces the relative they've left behind.

It's during moments like that when I really wish every single person in the world could see spirit the way I do. I genuinely believe that this world would be a more peaceful and forgiving place if everyone could actually see someone dear to them return from death and gently touch them, hold their hand, or even cuddle them as they reach through the mist that separates this life from the next.

Occasionally a spirit person will come through who isn't directly linked to the sitter though and will attempt to relay messages to their own family on this side of life. This can be an old neighbour or acquaintance who is often unknown to the person at the time or family member. When that situation arises I always leave it up to the person who has visited me to decide if they want to pass on the communication or not. Most times they will.

I call these spirits 'drop-in spirits'. This may be their only chance of telling their loved ones here that they are happy so when someone very distantly related in some way to them visits a psychic or medium, they'll try to gatecrash the sitting and attempt to get their tuppence-worth in – and who can blame them?

My own limited view of the spirit world has shown me that it really seems to be a genuinely beautiful place, where people are happy after they cross over and are reunited with long-dead family members and acquaintances, and it seems the only worry they have is for the people left behind in this life.

It seems to be a place that is without any physical suffering whatsoever and after the soul has been emotionally healed, it's said there are jobs to be done over there too. So it isn't simply a life of leisure as communities still exist and have to be maintained. I realise how strange this must sound and even I have trouble getting my head round the concept of an afterlife that in any way resembles this life we are all living, but I'll take their word for it because I haven't been there myself to disagree!

When someone from the spirit world attempts to 'come through' to a medium, I'm told it is not an easy process for them. They use an awful lot of energy (and so does the medium) so it just goes to show how much love they have for their loved ones here as they attempt to communicate.

Throughout my own experiences I've seen many instances and heard numerous stories about love continuing after the death of a physical body and I'm honoured to be able to share a couple of those stories with you here.

A psychic reading is a very private moment for a sitter and I always keep everything said during any reading 100 per cent confidential, but if some of the stories that unfold are uplifting and can help another person through the grief and heartache of a life alone, then I think they are worth disclosing. I'd like to thank the people involved – both living and in spirit – for allowing me to include their personal and life-changing experiences here.

The Feather
This first experience I'll tell you about happened a few years back and still affects me deeply. I was approached by a young man and woman after one of my floorshows; the young man asked me if I ever performed healing for

people. I informed him that I very rarely attempted that kind of thing and offered them some numbers of reiki practitioners I knew of. They told me I had been to their house several years before and their little daughter, who was five at the time of my visit, thought I was really funny and liked me so they really wanted me and were willing to pay well. Although I was flattered I reminded them that I wasn't a healer and didn't possess those abilities. I had helped people with meditation and relaxation techniques in the past, but would never charge for that part of my work and had never worked with a young child before either, so I really didn't think I was the man for the job.

They remained adamant that I was the only person their wee girl wanted, so I reluctantly agreed to give it a try and we arranged a date for me to visit.

A few days later, I walked into the hospital ward and was greeted with the most beautiful smile from their wee girl as she lay on her bed, surrounded by cards and dolls. I instantly remembered her but was horrified to discover she had terminal cancer and the outlook was very bleak. She was only nine years old.

She was a wonderful wee soul whose positive outlook on the world and strength of character in such trying circumstances made me feel very humble indeed. She had been in hospital so many times and had endured all kinds of treatments but still remained upbeat and possessed an excellent sense of humour – mostly at my expense I might add.

I must admit I was devastated to sense this wee soul's passing was imminent but began to use visualisation techniques and crazy made-up stories to attempt to ease her discomfort and make her final moments in this life bearable. I visited her a few times that week and spent hours with her parents as they told me stories about her and how well she did at school before the illness . . . I soon began to look forward to our wee sessions.

One afternoon, I told her exhausted mum and dad to take a wee break and grab a coffee while I began one of my daft stories that made her relax and smile. As I began, she stopped me mid-sentence.

'I had a dream last night Tom,' she quietly whispered.

'I hope it was a nice one?' I replied.

'It was amazing. In my dream my Gran and Grandpa came on a big white dove from heaven.' She smiled as she relived the dream in her mind.

'That sounds a nice dream,' I said, as a sense of sadness and dread washed over me.

'It was great,' she said. 'They said I can fly with the dove too when they come back for me next time . . . they said they'll take me to heaven and I can be an angel.'

By this time I was trying my best to hold back my tears.

'Tom, will my mum and daddy be OK when I'm in heaven?'

For once in my life, I was completely lost for words and was thankful when her parents walked back in the room.

'Here, don't you talk like that,' I said, trying to force a smile. 'You keep trying to get better . . . or you'll have me tae answer tae.'

She smiled as I continued with a silly story until she finally fell asleep, and as dusk fell on the world outside, she lay there in the dim light with her mum and dad gazing at their precious wee girl. I joined them in a quiet prayer for her and made my way home, and as I walked out the main entrance of the hospital I prayed again that she could be miraculously cured somehow.

I was due to visit again a few days later but one morning I received the phone call I had dreaded: she had slipped away the previous night.

I am ashamed to admit that I cursed the spirit world that day and felt so much anger that a wee girl with so much promise could be taken in such a way. I took a walk and sat in the park for a few hours watching the world go by as I pondered the meaning of this life and the next and why so many innocents suffer in this existence. Suddenly, my mobile phone rang and I saw it was her dad's number. I reluctantly answered. I was reluctant because at that moment I could not have given the couple any spiritual consolation at all, but I knew I couldn't let him down because *he* was the one needing comfort over the loss of his child.

He told me that he and his wife had finally got home from the hospital at 6 a.m. that morning after the wee one's passing. Exhausted and grief stricken they placed the key into the door of the dark empty house. As they climbed the stairs to their wee girl's room and entered they were shocked and surprised to see a single white feather lying on the pillow of her bed.

He asked me if I thought there was any significance to this as there was nothing in her room that it could have come from and they just couldn't understand how it had got there. Before I said a word to him, I stared up at the clear blue sky above and just knew her Gran and Grandpa had indeed come for her and heaven now had one more angel.

Life Is Wonderful

Another true story that I've been allowed to tell, centres around an old couple who were both in their eighties when they came to see me a while back. They had decided to see a psychic to attempt to hear something about their late son, who had tragically died forty years earlier at the age of fifteen. The woman was in a wheelchair and was being pushed by her frail husband. As we sat and I opened up the communication, I could sense the disappointment when he didn't come through to them. Sadly there are times when this happens and there's absolutely nothing I can do to force a spirit to come through. I can't lie to people just to make them happy, so it's very disappointing for all parties involved, including me – and this was one of those times.

A woman did come through and it became clear she was the lady's mother as she told us she was looking after her grandson in spirit but still, the old couple left the room a wee bit frustrated at not actually hearing from their boy . . . and I can completely understand why.

About two years later the man visited me again but this time he was alone. It didn't take a psychic to know what had happened in the period since I last saw him. His lovely wee wife had sadly died and he sought communication from both her and the boy now. I quietly begged the spirit world to please help them come through and ease the intense grief he was feeling as I began to open up for the attempt at communication.

I was overjoyed when, after a few moments, his wife appeared in front of my eyes but this time she was looking youthful and fresh (the way most people in spirit tend to look, I have to add). Her complexion looked great and her eyes were bright as she smiled broadly and mouthed the word 'hello' to me. I excitedly informed her eager husband that she was there beside him and, as the communication began to flow, his tears of sadness became tears of joy as they relived personal moments and held hands. To see such devotion and love transcend the barriers of physical death makes me realise how privileged I am and it makes the derision and ridicule from narrow-minded cynics who can never experience such a sight seem laughable to me.

As the communication continued that day, there was still no sign of their son coming through and I was getting concerned for his father beside me. I was thankful when a young man materialised a moment later and just as I was about to describe him to the sitter, he stared in disbelief at the sight of his son standing there, as real as life: he could see him too! I was ecstatically happy as I watched the young man interact with his teary-eyed dad. Although the boy didn't verbally communicate, the vision of him and the smile on his face and his actions must have made his father so happy. For someone to see the spirit form of a loved one during a reading is rare but when it happens the person is usually filled with joy, and any fear soon fades.

I sat back and let the three of them embrace, before the woman took her son's hand and they both began to fade. As she left us she smiled and said, 'We'll all be going to Sauchiehall Street together soon.' Then in a moment they were gone and we were alone in the room again. I passed on the strange message to the old man. He smiled as his eyes filled up again.

'I know what she's on about,' he said. 'We were due to take our boy to Sauchiehall Street in Glasgow to buy him a new jacket on the Tuesday but he died on the Monday, the day before we were due to go. He loved Sauchiehall Street.'

As he left the room that day feeling uplifted, he told me he felt so happy that the two most precious people in his life were reunited and was now looking forward to crossing over with them when his own time finally came.

A month or so later he phoned me and left a message on my answering machine saying he could now see his son in the house daily and could sense his wife too as she lay beside him at night. He went on to say that his radio had switched itself on one morning and 'What a Wonderful World' had been playing – this he said was his wife's favourite song and he was now completely convinced of an afterlife! He really was a happy man.

A week or so later I attempted to call him back several times and didn't receive a reply but thought no more of it. Another week had passed when I tried again but this time the telephone was answered by a very polite and rather stuffy-voiced woman. She informed me that he had passed away a few days earlier and the house was now being cleared.

I placed the phone down that day with a tinge of sadness and happiness; now he was with his beloved wife and son and would feel the pain of loneliness and grief no more. But I still felt a sense of melancholy as I thought of such a great character passing from this world.

About two years later I was walking through Glasgow city centre with my wife when I saw an old man, a woman and a young boy walking through the busy street and they were all looking directly at me! They seemed familiar . . . then I was sure it was that family! At first I thought my eyes were playing tricks until they turned and smiled at me as we passed them by.

'Hello Tom,' said the old man smiling happily as he passed me by.

I turned round to have another look but they had vanished amid the bustling throng of shoppers.

'Did ye see that there?' I asked my wife.

'See what?' she answered.

'Those three people that said hello to me. Did ye see them?' I asked.

'I didn't see anybody talk to you,' she said as she made her way to a shop window.

And guess what? I looked up at the street sign on the wall and there it was – how could I have forgotten? A Tuesday afternoon on Sauchiehall Street!

I know of many stories and events that have happened where spirit interact and give comfort to the living, but sadly it's all too few and far between, and there are many narrow-minded people out there who would laugh and mock someone who has experienced spiritual contact, simply because they haven't experienced such a thing. Some rational people I've met are afraid to tell others of their experiences for fear of ridicule but, believe me, the spirit world does exist and our loved ones are never far away, of that I'm convinced. If you, the reader disagree then that's your prerogative, but I feel honoured and blessed to have seen life continue in a higher realm and will always be comforted by the knowledge that this existence is only the beginning.

I have a real dislike for false psychics and mediums who charge ridiculous fees and prey on the grief stricken who are desperate for some kind of sign from their beloved family member or friend, so I'd like you to read the next bit carefully as I attempt a 'psychic experiment'. I really need your co-operation as I attempt something great.

The Reading

In this next section of the book I'm going to talk a little bit about *you* if that's OK? Yes *you*, reading this. If you feel uncomfortable with that then please skip this chapter and go to the next part . . . but I think you'll be surprised.

What I'm about to do here is something that has never been attempted before and it may fail – but I don't think it will. I'm sure it'll work and be quite accurate. I'm going to do the first psychic reading by print!

Sounds crazy, eh? Well, when this book went to print, I wrote thousands of different versions of this chapter . . . and this one is uniquely for *you*!

So, if you're ready, then let's begin.

OK, I feel you are quite a sensitive person who manages, somehow to cover it up in public . . . ?

You are quite good with other people and manage well but sometimes you really need to be alone and away from the world . . . ?

Your life seems to have taken a VERY different path from the one you originally wanted to take . . . why?

I'm getting the letter 'J' as I write this . . . ? It's a male I think . . . ? Can you take that . . . ? You MUST know who it is! A 'Jo' . . . 'James' . . . 'or a 'Jay' sound?

I'm seeing water around you . . . do you live near a river, a lake, a well, or is there water running near you?

Who has the silver-coloured car . . . ?

I must say I don't like what I'm seeing around work for you . . . ? You aren't appreciated at work are you . . . ?

You need to stay healthy because other people rely on you . . .

I keep getting the letter 'J' again . . . a male . . . ? A funny character . . . ? Alive or dead . . . ? THINK ABOUT IT OR ASK SOMEONE CLOSE TO YOU, OK!

In your future I see you visiting overseas and finally trying to take some well-deserved rest.

The number six is important too! Very lucky!

I'm also seeing news of a wedding coming up . . . ?

. . . and a birth!

Thank you. Bless.

Well, how did we do then? What percentage of the reading was correct? I really hope it worked because this was a unique experiment and was uniquely for *you*.

OK . . . sorry to tell you it was all bunkum! Some of you may have come to that conclusion already. It was a variation of a technique called cold reading that has been used for years by fake psychics and magicians to fool the gullible. Sadly, we are all gullible to an extent and enjoy hearing about ourselves. (Even me!) I'll guarantee at least fifty per cent of you reading this felt it applied to you.

Let's go through the 'reading' again and this time I'll explain how they trick us.

OK, I feel you are quite a sensitive person who manages somehow to cover it up in public . . .

(Every one of us has some degree of sensitivity and we all pretend to be tougher to the outside world than we really are – it's a basic part of our survival.)

You are quite good with other people and manage well but sometimes you really need to be alone and away from the world . . . ?
(There is less of a chance of a 'hit' with this one because some of us aren't too good with other people but if the fake reader gets it correct the poor sitter can be quite impressed. And who doesn't feel the need to have more time alone now and again?)

Your life seems to have taken a VERY different path from the one you originally wanted to take . . . why?
(If you can remember your hopes, dreams and ambitions as a youth, I'm sure they're different from the life you live now. It's very rare for any of us to be living the life we originally dreamed of.)

I'm getting the letter 'J' as I write this . . . ? It's a male I think . . . ? 'J' . . . ? Can you take that? You MUST know who it is! A 'Jo' . . . 'James' . . . or a 'Jay' sound?
(I'm sure we all know a man connected to the letter 'J'. I can think of four people straight away. Notice how I've questioned you and then bullied you into remembering. This is something I've witnessed many times. If a 'psychic' shows extreme confidence, and even touches of aggression, then there is more of a chance the poor recipient will do his or her best to agree.)

I'm seeing water around you . . . Do you live near a river, a lake, a well or is there water running near you?
(Good chance there's water near your house somewhere.)

Who has the silver-coloured car . . . ?
(Nowadays a huge percentage of the population has a silver car! Just look around the next time you're in a car park and see for yourself.)

I must say I don't like what I'm seeing around work for you . . . ? You aren't appreciated at work are you . . . ?
(Most of us feel like that relating to our work . . . even psychics!)

You need to stay healthy because other people rely on you
. . .
(True . . . but not a psychic message, unless you interpret it as one.)

I keep getting the letter 'J' again . . . ? A male . . . ? A funny character . . . ? Alive or dead . . . ? THINK ABOUT IT OR ASK SOMEONE CLOSE TO YOU, OK!
(Back to that again. Chances are the sitter will have thought of someone by this time but this type of approach will make any person feel awkward. I know I'm being a big bully, sorry. If you keep racking your brains you'll think of someone of course . . . and notice how I've added 'alive or dead' to widen the chances. In the end, I've taken the easy way out and left the question with the poor sitter. This is very common with fakers.)

*In your future I see you visiting overseas and finally trying
to take some well-deserved rest.*
(Can't argue with the future – the 'psychics' can say what
they want here.)

The number six is important too! Very lucky!
(It might be. Who knows? The 'psychic' doesn't.)

I'm also seeing news of a wedding coming up . . . ?
(I'm sure there will be . . . sometime in the future . . . for
someone we know.)

And a birth!
(I'm sure there will be . . . that's life.)

So, as you can see, cold reading can be used to con gullible
people and if someone tries to fool you with this
nonsense, tell them you know their wee evil secret and it
was me who told you! I personally don't have any problem
with someone who isn't a psychic doing a wee harmless
fortune telling for fun as *long as they tell the customer it's
for entertainment and isn't real.* What I do have a problem
with is unscrupulous fakes trying to con people who are
gullible or desperate and giving the rest of us a bad name.
Believe me, a con artist using this junk can really mess
some innocent people's lives up.

I promise you that if you visit a real psychic who has a
genuine link with spirit your readings will be far more
personal and accurate than any magician or fraudulent
con artist could ever dream of, so tread carefully in the
'field' of psychics and mediums; there is an awful lot of
dung.

I notice that when a person walks in for a reading they may be smiling and look as if they are there purely for fun but they are usually taking on board everything the psychic or medium is telling them. It is therefore very important for the psychic to be careful what they say and how they say it.

I've been visited numerous times by people who have been told some horrific news about their future by unscrupulous charlatans who don't care about people's feelings and only want a wee bit of glory and money. Many genuine psychics I know have had to repair a lot of emotional damage caused by eejits who have bought tarot cards and preyed on the gullible.

If you are one of the many who have decided to develop your intuition and work with spirit, then be prepared for life to change dramatically for you. Anyone dedicating their life to spirit communication or psychic work is going to be in for a very difficult time, both emotionally and mentally. For instance, if you become a professional psychic and become popular, either locally or nationally, when someone is first introduced to you and informed about your work, they will either treat you with suspicion, ridicule, fear, admiration or even downright aggression. You are no longer treated as the person you really are and this can take a while to get used to.

You will be challenged by drunks to prove your abilities in public or will be harassed at parties or evenings out by people wanting a reading from you. For instance, as my wife lay in the throes of labour at 4 a.m., the midwives on the maternity ward asked me to leave her lying there and do some readings for them next door. Unlike most jobs, you are *always* expected to perform.

You will have to become thick skinned and be tougher with people in general and know when to say no without being rude. Giving some drunken person a free reading at a party or in a club because they begged you to is not respectable to spirit and is wrong, believe me . . . and they won't thank you for it either. I used to do it all the time but nowadays I politely tell the person that I'm not working, the 'lines are closed' and I would need some time to prepare anyway. And if they keep on harassing me? Well, let's just say I tell them where to go to. If they really want a reading let them visit you in a professional setting.

Some people, even in the spiritualist world, think it is terrible to charge a fee for psychic readings. I totally disagree with this and personally think psychics should charge something for their time and effort. The fee shouldn't be too expensive of course but I believe it should at least be the equivalent to a fee charged by hairdressers or therapists.

Why do I think psychics should charge? Well, for a start everyone has a right to charge for their time and effort and we all have bills to pay and if the customers don't like it then they can look elsewhere for someone who works for free, simple as that. To read a few people in an evening is extremely tiring and drains the psychic of so much energy and, I believe, merits some form of compensation, but these are only my own thoughts.

Some psychics accept 'donations' and if you are financially stable enough to be able to give your time either for free or a small donation then good for you, but sadly most of us can't afford either the time or the money to read for free. I used to only work for free until word of mouth spread and I had the difficult choice to either give it all up and keep doing my 'normal' job or charge for my services. I'd honestly make more money with a normal job, so please don't think you'll become rich working as a psychic . . . you probably won't!

Now, please notice I am talking about *psychic* readings above. This type of reading covers tarot, crystals, runes, palmistry etc., where the reader attempts to help the sitter and tries to tap into their life path for them using clairvoyance. Using your abilities as a *medium* (i.e. contacting spirit) is different in my personal view and I always try and fit in some time every week to help families contact their loved ones and I don't charge a single penny for this at all. If they desperately want to give me a donation I direct them to the nearest charity box! I look at my free medium sessions as a payback for the help that the spirit world has given me during my psychic readings.

I suppose it's up to every individual but if you decide to read people for a fee, please don't rip anyone off – you'll lose any ability you develop and your reputation, and that of many others, will be tarnished if you do. But don't undercharge either, because people will treat you as a three-quid psychic if that's what you charge. It's entirely up to you.

Some people question why anyone should charge for 'God's work' but God gives a lot of people abilities – electricians, psychologists, counsellors, carpenters etc. – and every one of them gets paid and I believe that psychics should too, simple as that. We eat too!

I have to admit that I disappoint several people a week who come for a private sitting. The reason for this is that I totally refuse to lie and make nonsense up just to please people at the time, and as I said earlier, it sometimes just doesn't happen. It can be like having a mobile phone and no reception.

It is a fact that you will have clients that cannot be read. This can be for several reasons: (A) there just isn't a connection for them and the 'lines are closed'; (B) they are totally unresponsive and refuse to cooperate; (C) they don't believe and are there for a laugh at you; or (D) they're too nervous!

If anyone comes to see me and I can't get a connection for them for any of the reasons above I refuse to even attempt to continue. I can usually tell straight away from the moment they walk in the room. When this happens the person is always surprised and disappointed at this and occasionally they'll think I've 'seen something bad' for them. I explain to them that I've seen absolutely nothing negative at all and it's nothing to worry about but they always leave feeling disappointed or even angry. But hey, they'll get over it and end up thanking me for being honest.

But just imagine how disappointed they would be if I sat and told them a load of nonsense I'd made up just to please myself or to keep them happy and took a fee for it? They would go home and tell everyone they knew I was a useless psychic, they'd feel ripped off, I'd feel terrible for lying to them and my abilities would probably suffer.

So, I refuse point-blank to waste their time. I also refuse to sit and 'prove myself' to a sceptic who will not cooperate with a *yes* or *no* or argue with someone who is closed off. And if 'spirit says no' I say no.

I learned all the pitfalls the hard way years ago and hopefully telling you here will prevent anyone interested in genuinely working with spiritual and psychic connections from making the same mistakes I made as a boy. Spirits can't perform at the drop of a hat and occasionally they don't play by the rules so please . . . always tell the truth.

Is there another job in the world where some of the audience don't believe you, others want you to tell them everything about themselves, and the rest are terrified of you? A job where you are reuniting long-lost loved ones one day and running from terrifying evil entities the next? That is the weird and wonderful life of a psychic and medium . . . a strange life indeed.

9

GETTING IN TUNE

OK, if you've reached this far in the book I guess you may genuinely be interested in psychic phenomena and possibly developing any abilities you feel you may have. Or maybe you already have developed your senses before and want to visit some active locations yourself? Some of you may even fancy 'trying it out' just to see if anything happens. Well, just like any other aspect of psychic phenomena, I can't guarantee results but I can equip you with the mind tools I use to develop your natural senses, and like so many others who have used these techniques before you, the results can work very well. But . . . nothing comes for free. Don't worry I'm not going to ask you to send me money. What I would like you to do is give 100 per cent though.

Some people I meet after my public demonstrations, who are involved in the spiritualist community, tell me they are a 'developing' medium or 'developing' psychic, and then usually ask me how they can 'develop' their abilities faster.

I always have the same answer: I'm a 'developing' medium and psychic too!

I have no quick answers or special abilities and can offer no sure-fire, quick route to becoming an excellent medium or psychic and, believe me, no one can. What I can offer them is some advice, some tried and tested meditation and visualisation techniques and an honest account of my own development through the years that can maybe help them avoid the pitfalls I experienced along this long, weird and wonderful journey I've taken. But until the day all spirit communication comes through as clear as a phone call to me, then I'll class myself as a developing medium too.

Before we continue, I have to tell you right here and now that I personally believe there is no exact way to develop your psychic abilities. I've read many books on the subject and have seen an awful lot of nonsense along with good practical advice within the pages of each publication. And it doesn't matter if the psychic 'teacher' is a TV star or takes to the platform at the local spiritualist church once a month, all subjects who want to increase their natural abilities will respond to different development techniques and if the exercises and guidance are wrong for them, then they may never reach their full potential.

For instance, someone who is very doubtful by nature but thinks they may have something to develop will probably scoff at being told to look for an angel or see a person's aura at the beginning of their spiritual journey. This kind of visual experience may – and probably will – occur later for them but at the outset they may become disheartened with all this 'airy-fairy' talk and give up.

However, someone who has an inherent deep spiritual belief would be far more open to the same suggestions and wouldn't question the possibility of seeing auras and angels. In fact, they may have experienced something like this before, and so their first stages of learning will be very different from the former. Being a convinced believer surprisingly does not mean one person will spiritually grow faster or be *more psychic* than the other, but the more rational minded person has to be guided differently. For complete sceptics who think people like me are either con men or crazy, as you can guess, there's usually no hope.

I imagine a huge percentage of people reading this book will have at least some interest in the spirit world but, for a moment, I'd like you to just visualise yourself as someone who has been rather sceptical of all things esoteric throughout your life and suddenly, while in your fifties, your life changes and you begin to receive premonitions and hear discarnate voices. You would definitely think you were going mad. Well, this happened to Bill, a gentleman who reluctantly came to see me a few years back.

He had been a lawyer all his life and had to take early retirement due to severe heart problems and arthritis. It was during a heart attack in his kitchen when Bill swore he saw a blinding white light and a man with white robes appear in front of him. Thankfully the attack proved not to be fatal and he woke up in hospital a few hours later. He admitted he was rather puzzled about his experience but, being the sceptical soul he was, put it all down to some kind of hallucination caused by the attack.

A few weeks had passed when he began to hear voices when he was all alone. At first they were quite faint, like inaudible whispers, but soon they became clearer and would sound strangely familiar on occasion. He was then beginning to *feel* things about people he'd meet and have intense urges to tell them information about themselves, even though he really didn't want to.

Needless to say, he was a very worried and confused man by the time I met him.

When he walked in the door to see me that afternoon, he looked me up and down cautiously and proceeded to sit down in front of me. His guarded behaviour reminded me of the moment two animals meet and circle each other suspiciously. His son had set up the meeting for him so I was informed of all the details of his reason for visiting me beforehand and there was to be no reading or guesswork on my part. With the pleasantries and introductions over I decided to find out more.

'So, you've been having psychic experiences then?' I asked.

'Well, if you want to call them that,' he laughed. 'I personally think I'm going off my head but my son thinks I should come to you. To be honest I don't know why I'm here. I feel a bit silly.'

'What's been happening?' I asked.

'Well, I keep hearing these bloody voices and I keep feeling I've just got to tell people things.'

At this, he sat back and smiled at how ridiculous this all sounded, even to him.

'Look, I class myself as one of the most rational people about, Tom. I honestly don't believe in this kind of nonsense . . . nae offence, but I just can't fathom out what's been happening to me. Am I mad? I even went to the doctor wondering if I had a brain tumour or something like that but I got the all clear. I was wondering if I was schizophrenic.'

'Are these messages you're receiving accurate and do they mean something for the people they're meant for?' I asked.

'Aye, sometimes they're really spooked out! They must think I'm some psycho who's been doing detective work about them!'

'Welcome to the psychic world, Bill,' I said to him.

He burst out laughing in my face. I then explained to him that no one is more sceptical than me but if something seems very real to you, you are medically clear and the information can be validated personally or publicly by someone, then there must be some basis of reality in the experience. I told him how I've been given proof of life after death and witnessed psychic phenomena numerous times and will always 'fight the cause' but could understand his viewpoint, coming from such a rational and analytical life as a lawyer for so many years.

I then said he was welcome to come to me again if he wanted and he agreed to learn more – 'out of curiosity'. I worked with Bill a few times afterwards and he developed his gift at a reasonable rate but I will tell you here and now, it was *very* hard work for me. He always needed definitive proof and the only way he could find that kind of proof was by opening up his mind – but his mind was closed from the beginning. It felt like a Catch 22 situation and I occasionally felt I was in court, on a witness stand for the defence of the spirit world.

He questioned everything I tried to explain to him and argued the rational side of any experience he felt until one day, it finally happened . . . his eyes were opened to the world of spirit . . . in his bath of all places! He claimed he saw his mother in front of him in and she spoke clearly to him and he was sure it was definitely no hallucination. After that day his abilities blossomed. And now? Well, you probably think I'm going to tell you he's now a medium or healer or something? No, today Bill potters about his garden and simply accepts his gift and if something *strange* happens then he just shrugs it off. He has absolutely no urge to become a professional psychic or give spiritual messages to strangers any more but he says he is now more prepared for the afterlife and can have some control over 'the voices'.

In Bill's opinion, most psychics are, to say the least, eccentric and some of our beliefs and practices may seem off the wall to someone like him. But after a while I believe even the moderate sceptical individuals can create their own pathways to spiritual fulfilment. As long as they open their mind up a little. It just takes a little longer.

Now, Cathy was a completely different case: she believed in EVERYTHING! Fairies, elves, goblins, mermaids, ghosts, and, of course psychics, you name it and she believed in it.

Now, I have to admit I worry about people like Cathy. To believe in everything that has been reported as paranormal or mystical without any real evidence, although harmless, can cause others to think you are a little bit crazy. And to link spirit communication, psychic phenomena and the like with fairies and elves etc. doesn't fit with my personal beliefs. (Who knows I may be wrong.)

Cathy had been at some of my live demonstrations and obviously felt impressed enough to join a development group I was hosting a few months later. As she entered the room that morning she shouted something about 'the energies' being all wrong and proceeded to set off the building's fire alarm with some burning sage she was wafting about the room. A great start.

After fifteen minutes in the freezing car park, we returned to the room where she then proceeded to tell the group that her spirit guide was the Native American chief, Sitting Bull and, wait for this, General Custer was Sitting Bull's butler in the spirit world. Cathy then gave a 'message' to someone in the group from her alleged 'guide'.

'Sitting Bull say, "you be careful driving car on motorway . . . me see burst tyre . . . "' Her stereotypical Native American accent, with a hint of Glasgow dialect caused ripples of stifled laughter throughout the room.

'I don't actually drive,' the poor victim replied.

'Sitting Bull say "your wife drive, not you." Sitting Bull say "you deaf as totem pole",' the great chief replied.

'I'm . . . I'm not married, sorry,' he said apologetically.

'Sitting Bull say . . . "you WILL be married in three years! Young wife, blue eyes, blonde hair, two little squaws . . . No argue with Sitting Bull, OK? Me, great warrior chief, you . . . wee stupid white man,"' she shouted as she opened her eyes and became Cathy again.

'Oh he just enters me whenever he wants,' she added as the group finally burst out laughing, much to her annoyance.

The poor recipient of his/her wisdom looked at the rest of us and silently mouthed the words 'I'm gay' as Sitting Bull finally left the building for a while – no doubt followed by his trusty butler, General Custer!

We, on the other hand, were left with his *spirit messenger* who then proceeded to chant some mantra and roll her eyes.

I knew I really had trouble ahead and considered quietly asking Cathy to leave. But, hey, man, she'd turned up and was, to say the least, enthusiastic so I thought I'd give it a go.

Throughout that day, and subsequent days of the course, I had many disagreements with Cathy and her guide. I am open to all possibilities from spirit but some of the rubbish that her guide allegedly uttered was usually unconsciously funny and occasionally quite dangerous. For instance, he told several members of the group the date and exact time they would be 'crossing over' to meet their maker! When I confronted her, I was greeted with staring eyes and a loud 'How' and told my own date for dying too. Let's just say if the great chief was correct in his calculations, I wouldn't be sitting here writing this now.

I've found there can be a definite fine line between some people's alleged psychic experiences and sheer madness, and I was sure at that moment that Cathy's abilities were caused by the latter. So, I politely asked her to leave the group, gave her the fee she'd paid and the rest of us carried on productively and peacefully for the rest of the course.

It wasn't until a few months later that she contacted me again but this time I told her straight that I thought her behaviour was definitely not conducive to a peaceful atmosphere where people can develop and informed her that I wasn't sure if she *was* psychic. I could sense this was making her very angry, but deep down she couldn't deny it rang true. Some people have come up to me at parties and pubs, drunk, and proceeded to inform me they are 'more psychic' than me and gone on to give strangers around vague ridiculous 'messages', but most of the time they simply do it for the attention and their egos get in the way. To work with spirit we must respect others and only give messages if the living person wants them . . . not because the drunk 'psychic' wants to impress.

Anyway, back to Cathy. She finally apologised and explained how she always felt nervous in a group setting and just had to perform in front of people and thinking back, felt embarrassed at her behaviour that day. This seemed to be a very different woman I was talking to on the phone. So, after some negotiating we agreed that she could come and talk to me at least.

A few days later she turned up at my door, wearing a multi-coloured kaftan and a fez hat. After drinking coffee and talking for an hour or so, I realised that sitting in front of me was a highly intelligent, caring and witty woman, with extremely strong psychic abilities, who just happened to be a little bit eccentric. I found out her background was in amateur theatre so, as you can imagine, she did like to 'perform' whenever the chance arose. During our conversation, I had picked up from my guide that she had been abused as a child and had created imaginary friends to help her through each day. Her only break from her abuser was her weekend visits to the cinema to watch western movies, where she always rooted for the 'Indians' and booed the cowboys. This was all validated by her and we agreed to try again. As you can see it doesn't take a psychology degree to understand the origins of her spirit guide and behaviour.

The next development day came and Cathy entered, as loud and dramatic as ever but willing to develop and join in the group. She blossomed beyond belief and at some stages astonished everyone present with her psychic results during the exercises. With Sitting Bull and General Custer safely out of the way, she became loved and admired by everyone present, including the author here.

When I contacted her to read this piece I'd written before I published it, she was living alone in a cottage in the highlands of Scotland, caring for injured hedgehogs and other wildlife. She claims she can hear the trees talking and can find out what is wrong with the creatures simply by listening to what the trees tell her. (I've written about animal communication in a previous chapter.) She also says she sees fairies and elves in her garden at night and is ecstatically happy at their visits and even leaves out fruit for them! She says that her real spirit guide is a young Native American woman.

To some people, Cathy may sound a bit off the wall. Two years ago I may have agreed but now I think she has genuine psychic abilities which I've witnessed first-hand and is one of life's great colourful characters who brighten up this drab grey world we live in. Who knows, maybe the fairies and elves in her garden are real; they definitely are to her and simply because I haven't experienced these things definitely doesn't mean they don't exist. Who am I to question? As I've said before, my life's work seems very odd to some. I have to say though, in my opinion Cathy is now a very gifted psychic because, just like Bill, she opened up her mind. And, like everyone we meet in this, the physical life, I learned as much about myself from her as she did from me.

With all due respect for the real Native American chief, thank goodness Cathy's Sitting Bull and his spirit butler, General Custer, rode off into the sunset.

OK then, for those of you reading this who would like to fine-tune your senses and attempt to pick up residual vibes from psychic hotspots, let's begin.

Remember, you have to believe in yourself and your abilities and try to not to analyse things too much. Your 'conscious' mind will try to analyse the situation so you have to try and let it have a wee nap, while your 'unconscious' mind can open up to the energies around you. It's also a good idea to try to place yourself somewhere that you won't be disturbed for a wee while. So, turn off any phones and put a notice on your door saying 'PSYCHIC DEVELOPMENT . . . KEEP OOT OR ELSE!' or something maybe a wee bit more subtle perhaps.

If you want, you can get up and walk away from your meditation at any stage, because you won't be sleeping, in a trance or anything like that but it works better if you can relax and take the time.

So, what next? Well let's try and arrange a little face-to-face meeting with your spirit guides and exercise your 'psychic muscles'.

RELAX!

OK, first of all I'd like you to sit back or lie down somewhere comfortable and reasonably peaceful. Now, kick off your shoes, put a cushion behind your head and try to make sure you won't be disturbed for a little while. This is *your* time, OK. Feel free to put some relaxing music on if you want.

With some practice you should be able to do this practically anywhere . . . and, whatever happens, the relaxation will be beneficial to you.

As you recline, your body will automatically relax a little bit, even if you still feel a little tense; the relaxation process has begun already and this tension will disappear very soon.

Normally I'd ask you to close your eyes at this point but obviously you won't be able to read this with your eyes closed, (if you can then you definitely don't need this book!) so I'd like you to try to memorise the points I've highlighted the next time you do this. But for now just lie back and read on.

I believe that to be able to transport ourselves towards genuine spiritual contact we have to be able to understand the material world in which we live and discover the boundaries that exist between here and the next life. Always remember we are only a heartbeat away from the afterlife and our time spent in the physical shell (our body) is a learning curve for most of us. Human nature causes us to adapt to our environment and, in turn, take our lives and surroundings for granted but for once I'd like you to try to view the world differently.

Now, I'd like you to use your imagination for a moment.

As you sit or lie in comfort I'd like you to imagine you are a new-born child and have never felt anything in this material world before. (I know this might sound strange but bear with me.) First, **breathe in slowly**. As you take a deep breath of air in I'd like you to imagine that was your first experience of this world and as your lungs fill with life just think what it would be like to **appreciate every breath**. In this life we fail to appreciate the beauty of the natural things we have until they are taken away from us, so for now let's continue as a 'new born'.

I'd like you to **sink back** into the chair or bed you are on . . . feel how your limbs and torso are being supported by the chair . . . feel your neck and head sinking into the cushion behind you as you breathe slowly. **Imagine this**

was your first feeling of comfort like this. Now try and imagine the human energies connected to that piece of furniture under you. Visualise it being made from scratch and **think of all the people who have sat on it once or touched it in the past.** If it's yours, you'll probably know already, but if you go back even further to the first moment it was placed together by someone, I guess there will be other psychic imprints – try and imagine them.

Are there any pictures in your mind? If not don't worry, just keep relaxing. And now your energy is on it too . . .

Some of you may be thinking, 'Hey Tom, it's just a piece of furniture.' That is true I suppose but like everything in this material world, we take it all for granted. If you had never lain or sat on a piece of furniture like that before, it would be the most pleasurable experience you could imagine.

Now, if you can physically hear, listen to the natural sounds around you and allow yourself to relax a little bit more. **First, take a long deep breath . . . and exhale.**

Now, I'd like you to **imagine** all the skin in your **scalp relaxing** . . . now move on down over your **face**, imagine your **jaw and temples of your head relaxing** . . . now your **neck** (this area tightens with everyday stress; imagine your neck becoming relaxed) . . . then your **shoulders**; allow them to **sink** into a **deep relaxation** and enjoy . . . now your **chest** and **back** . . . take **another deep breath** and . . . **exhale** again. Think of your **lungs** blowing out all the stress of everyday life as your **chest**, **back** and **stomach** sink further into where you are . . . now your **arms**, all the way down to your **fingertips**; allow them to **relax** . . . now, imagine your **thighs** becoming **relaxed** . . . then your **calves** (this area carries a lot of stress too so allow it all to go now) . . . and finally, all the way down to your **feet** . . . allow them to **relax** . . . every muscle in **each foot** that takes so much pressure from most of us daily . . . can **relax**.

(You can go through the above relaxation method over and over again and you may have noticed I've highlighted some key words so you don't have to read the entire segment again. Just read the highlighted text next time and start at your scalp and keep working your way down.)

OK, I'd like you to now **visualise a staircase** in your mind's eye. At the **top** of the staircase is a **closed door** . . . the staircase has **ten ascending steps** . . . I'd like you to begin to **walk up the steps . . . one . . . two . . . three . . . four . . . five . . . six . . . seven . . . eight . . . nine . . . ten. Stand at the doorway** now, reach out and **turn** the **handle . . . open** the door . . . **step inside** . . . now imagine you're in a **room filled with light** . . . in the middle of the room there are **two chairs** and at the other side of the room is a window . . . imagine that through that window is the **vast landscape of life** . . . through that window is **the past, the present and the future** all **merging into one** . . . imagine at the other side of that window there are **no confines of space and time** . . . **no death**, only **everlasting life** in a different form. Now please **walk over** to the window . . . now **gaze** through the glass . . . **what do you see?**

Now, **step back** from the window and imagine the **light that is filling the room** covers your body and makes you feel **relaxed and happy**. Allow yourself to be **protected by the love of your guides** as you allow your **natural psychic abilities** to develop. These loving beings that guide us all will only allow pure and benevolent forces to influence us.

Now, please **take a seat** on one of the chairs. As the **beautiful light** in the room is **filling your mind** . . . think of your **guides** . . . they are around us . . . showing **love** and dedication to our earthly journey. Now ask them to help you to **open your mind** to the **natural** psychic **senses** we are all born with . . . once again, ask them to continue their **spiritual protection** throughout your physical life and to be there when you need them . . . ask them to give you courage, strength and a deeper love and understanding of all earthly beings and nature in this world . . . ask them to help you to glimpse the energies that separate the temporary physical world we live in with the everlasting life beyond.

Now, **stare at the chair in front of you**. Is there **anyone sitting opposite?** Remember, you are **surrounded by love and protection** at all times and absolutely **nothing negative** can ever happen to you as you follow your journey.

Take a few minutes if you like. This is your visualisation . . . **enjoy the relaxation** . . .

OK, **imagine yourself getting up and walking through the door**. It closes behind you as you begin to descend the steps, filled with light and love . . . **ten** . . . **nine** . . . **eight** . . **. seven** . . . **six** . . . **five** . . . **four** . . . **three** . . . **two** . . . **one** . . . as you 'return' to the physical world, allow that visual part of your mind to open up and sense the natural energies of everlasting life and nature that are all around us every day.

Now, open your eyes (if they were closed) and sit for a moment.

Now, I'd like you to look at the scene around you again, think of the chair or bed you are on and again try and sense the energies that have been involved in it from the beginning of its incarnation, all the way to you. Do you see or sense anything different about it now? If not, don't worry, just relax and chill out.

Try your best to perform this exercise a few times a week at least . . . you will feel the benefit in many ways. I always advise people to pick up everyday objects and try to 'feel' the information flowing from them.

Just remember that developing your intuition isn't a test. Everyone develops at their own pace and just because one person may develop faster than another doesn't mean that person will have the strongest senses in the long run. Just remember to relax and allow your mind to tune in to the world around you.

I believe that psychic development is similar to body-building. Just think, to build your muscles up you have to lift continuously heavier weights and eat the correct diet. Well, to develop your sensitivity you will have to start small and 'build up' and attempt to reach your limit too. When you've reached that limit – aim higher! There is no limit because you are unique. With a lot of hard work and concentration, you might hopefully be rewarded by a glimpse into the beautiful afterlife . . . and believe me, it's worth the effort.

Many people reach a plateau in their development and feel they can't achieve any more, but those are just the limitations of the human mind and you *can* develop further if you want; it might take a little time or a long time though so be patient. When I was younger I reached a very psychically active stage in my life where I saw and communicated with spirit everywhere and would try and read anyone at the drop of a hat! But still I wasn't happy and became angry if I couldn't be 100 per cent accurate all the time and as my life went on I realised that I was practically living in a haze of spiritual contact and had neglected my own loved ones in this side of life. I was also a complete nervous wreck and was constantly exhausted because I believed (wrongly) that all the premonitions and messages for people I received were actually coming from *me*! I then decided to close down the contact and in turn lost some of the ability for a year or two but, as I grew up a bit, learned about and embraced my guides, the communication began to slowly flow through again, and this time things were much more controlled and I have to say since that time have usually been good. So, try not to make the same mistake I made and force connections – if it doesn't happen then just move on. It'll all be fine.

With a wee bit of practice you'll be able to perform the above meditation and visualisation off by heart, anywhere. So, if you do decide to visit an allegedly haunted or active location, please remember to ask your guides for protection beforehand . . . in some places you will need it.

When you enter a spiritually active area with others, take a few moments to yourself, away from the rest of the group, to listen out for any spiritual information; close your eyes and just listen. Try to separate your mind as you hear the sounds of the living surrounding you but also try and listen to your 'outer thoughts'. What's an outer thought? Well, for a moment I'd like you to analyse a thought in your head. Are the words of the thought being spoken in your own inner voice? Now, imagine for a moment that the thought was emanating from *outside* your mind. Sometimes outer thoughts have different dialects or even languages from our own and give incredibly accurate messages . . . and sadly sometimes it's just gobbledygook! But when you hear an outer thought, listen closely to it and you never know, you might be surprised at the accuracy of this 'thought' and sometimes while listening you might hear the voices of spirit when you've developed more.

Quite often I see the dead in front of my eyes but most of the time I only hear them and sense them, so take any psychic information you are given and analyse it rationally before making any claims. With enough practice you'll soon distinguish between your own thoughts and the outer thoughts I mentioned earlier . . . and if you begin to see spirit like I do, then there will be absolutely no doubt in your mind that the information is otherworldly.

I believe our spiritual abilities and intuition have become practically obsolete in the modern Western world due to technology and science making life easier for us, so we all have a lot of work to do before we can convince everyone that these abilities do exist.

For instance, I'd like you to picture this:

It's a Friday night . . . you are a wee Scottish person, thousands of years ago, walking through any city street and looking for some grub . . . the only difference is there are no city streets . . . only forests and fields. You've been on the go for a very long time and are now feeling tired and hungry as you hunt for your next meal for your anxious family back home . . . and you have to be really careful because of the many big bears and wolves out there that are as hungry as you! Your senses are heightened as you see a small animal in a clearing . . . as you creep up to spear the poor thing, a big bear is quietly creeping up behind you . . . as you throw your spear, you hear a big roar, turn round and . . . well, you get the picture. Our ancestors had to use their intuition to survive.

Now, let's compare that to an awful lot of modern day Scottish people:

Friday night, thousands of years later . . . you creep into the kitchen and see nothing that takes your fancy . . . the family are fighting amongst themselves, so you decide to take the lead and go forage and hunt for . . . the local take away menus! Your senses are heightened slightly as you hold the menus in your hands . . . Indian? Chinese? Pizza? Or will it be fish 'n' chips tonight? You then pick up the phone and hold it in your hand like a spear and dial . . . you order, sit back down on your bahookey and watch a DVD as you wait for the doorbell to ring with your 'kill'.

Not exactly taxing the intuitive senses, but I think you'd agree, a whole lot easier, safer and enjoyable.

What I'm trying to say is that I believe our senses are dulled and lazy with technology, and that to develop and fine-tune a deeper understanding and connection to the spirit world in modern times, we have to go back to nature, the way our ancestors did. We are also up against radio waves, electricity currents and mobile phone signals nowadays, all of which I've found seem to interfere with psychic energies, so getting great accuracy is a hard job and it takes a whole lot of work and patience.

Whether you want to learn and devote your life's work as a psychic or simply want to begin a new stage in your own spiritual journey, practise the short meditation and ask your guides to help you along the way and, in my experience, it helps.

To be in tune with spirit energies and the world around you is an immense feeling and to be able to see and understand the ebb and flow of the world so clearly is a unique gift from above and, with enough practice, anyone can experience it . . . even me.

10

FOREVER YOUNG

As we near the end of our wee journey together, I hope I've given you a wee insight into the weird and wonderful life I've led throughout the years and some of the work and situations I've been involved in.

Some people will think I'm mad, others will say I'm a liar and the rest . . . well, I hope I've shown that even a big Glesga bampot like myself can open up and work for the spirit world and see the glorious life that lies ahead for the good and the just among us.

Working as a psychic medium, I've seen sadness and happiness in equal measure. I've seen lovers reunited through spirit after fifty years apart and witnessed sons speaking to long-dead fathers they never knew. I've watched rooms fill with spirit people who want to capture a precious moment with those they left behind and quietly shed a tear as people I know and love walked through the mists of death, hand in hand with spirit beings who love them eternally and will care for them. The loss of a loved one hurts a medium too.

The most difficult connections that I have ever experienced, though, are the passing away of the young.

As I've already touched on earlier in the book, the death of a child is the most devastating blow a family can have. To lose a mother, father, spouse or sibling is heartbreaking of course, but when death takes something so young and precious away from this world, the cycle of life and death is broken and the heartache is immense.

Many people (including me) question why babies and youngsters die but it seems there is no rhyme or reason when it comes to physical death and we are all at its mercy, no matter what age we are.

When a child comes through in a sitting, it is an incredibly emotional time for all involved but surprisingly the youngster in spirit is usually very happy and has no desire to return to their earthly body. They always seem to be looked after well and simply wait patiently for their earthly family to naturally pass over and join them when their time finally comes. They also regularly play alongside other living children they are related to.

On the odd occasion, I've witnessed children who are lost. For instance, in a haunted location they can usually be guided quite easily to 'the light' and finally to rest with their waiting loved ones from long ago.

After working as a psychic medium for many years I must say I was initially surprised at the number of young people and children who come through. When I first began readings, I imagined that I'd mostly be communicating with deceased elderly people in spirit but was shocked and upset when I saw so many young souls who never had the chance to grow up here in this side of life. My main spirit guide, William, died when he was a very young man in the First World War.

I've also noticed that people in spirit change very little and the essence of their personality survives intact. One example springs to mind.

I was lying in bed one night when a young girl appeared in front of me and asked to speak to a woman in this life. I quietly told her that she should visit me the next evening as I performed my readings and maybe that particular lady would be there – and I reminded her that it was 3 a.m. and I was trying to have a kip! She then giggled and evaporated as I conked out back to sleep.

The next evening a woman came to see me whose name matched the girl's request and was desperate to hear from her daughter. When I told her about the visitation the previous night and described the girl in detail she validated the information. The only problem was, the spirit girl hadn't turned up! Both of us were quite perturbed that she hadn't appeared and as the reading went on I saw her poor mum was becoming increasingly distraught at the possibility that she couldn't connect with her girl. Thankfully, just as the lady was leaving, her young daughter appeared and so began a long and emotional connection between the two. It turned out the girl, who was in her late teens when she passed away in a tragic road accident, was a terrible timekeeper in this life . . . and it seems the next. Thankfully she made it just in time that night.

Another experience that comes to mind is of a little boy who was four years old when he passed. He came through to his dad, tickled the bloke's nose and promptly threw a glass across the room! Why? Well, he just liked to scare people in this life whenever he got a chance. He was a real wee joker in this life and it seemed he hadn't changed because he had frightened many visitors to the family home out of sheer impishness. But the devotion the wee character had for his loved ones left behind caused him to make many return visits to his home, accompanied by his spiritual guardians.

People ask me if babies grow up on the other side. Well, in my experiences they do. Let me try and explain. During a spirit connection to a baby, I'm first shown a psychic impression of a baby – this is the spirit world trying to tell me the soul passed over while the physical body was a baby. Then, the spirit form usually manifests in front of me; sometimes they show themselves as having grown but I can honestly say I've never seen anyone in spirit who died as a baby look older than age twenty-one. Believe me, the years seem to be good to people who connect to us from the afterlife and, as I've said before, even people who may have looked terrible before their physical death, appear fresh faced and revived.

Anyway, back to spirit babies. I've been informed that the child is taken care of by the spiritual guardians I mentioned above – these are usually ancestors of the baby. As the child develops enough to understand, he or she is brought through in visitation to this side of life and introduced to his or her 'earthly' family. So it's said that when the loved ones finally pass over, they are greeted by the spiritual form of their lost children and are reunited at last.

My own wee granny lost four children in her lifetime and as anyone would imagine, never got over the loss, even many years later when I lived with her. So, when she finally passed over into spirit and came through one day, it was an amazing sight to behold as she sat in front of me, ecstatically happy, surrounded by her loving, long-lost kin. I realise all of this may sound idealistic and fanciful but I am now completely convinced we will all be reunited when we pass over and just enjoy spreading the word in this world!

An area that disturbs and worries many grieving families who believe in the world of spirit is the loss of someone through suicide. Yet again, these people who say 'animals have no soul' usually tell people that their loved one who has taken their own life will never reach the afterlife and will never be at rest.

This is complete nonsense . . . and *dangerous* nonsense at that!

Please believe me, if someone commits suicide they *will* be accepted into the loving realms of spirit. I know this because some people I knew over the years have chosen to take this tragic route and have revisited me since. I will admit that the transition seems to take a wee bit longer but I've found they will usually be at rest within a reasonably short while.

The reason they can take a little longer than a 'natural' passing is simple; they themselves find it difficult to move forward. Think of this: when a person commits suicide, it is the emotional equivalent to throwing a stone into water – the ripples are far reaching and the person usually realises the effect they've had on many people left behind and can have second thoughts. However, I'm told they are soon looked after by guides and the natural process of healing and development begins. So, if any of the 'spiritual rule makers' who spout this tripe tell you nonsense like that regarding one of your own . . . tell them where to go and walk away.

Although the spirit will be nurtured and the person cared for, the numerous people who have taken their own life who come through to their grief-stricken families are fine and well but I have to say they always regret their final actions and hurting those who love them in this life. I suppose it's just something they have to exist with on their conscience in the afterlife, but otherwise they'll be fine.

When death affects someone, I personally think they should consider visiting a grief counsellor before coming to see a medium. This may sound surprising to some, coming from me, but I think – in most cases – to move forward ourselves we have to let go of the person we have lost. Of course, we will always remember them and keep them close to our hearts, but to keep someone alive can be detrimental to the grieving process, I think, and it can be helpful to talk to someone.

However, visiting a reputable medium who can help bridge the gap between the two worlds and pass on accurate messages of love, happiness and forgiveness can also be beneficial to many too. I'd advise people not to visit mediums and psychics too often though, because they are only setting themselves up for a fall in the long run. We're dealing with a very unpredictable world when it comes to spirit. Many people, understandingly, refuse to let go of a beloved partner or family member and continue to visit mediums and psychics just to 'have a wee word' with their loved ones. Well, sadly the spirit world doesn't work to the same timetable and rules as we do and very often someone who has received a fantastic initial connection will be disappointed when they go to a medium again and the person they wanted can fail to come through for the third or fourth sitting. This doesn't mean the person in spirit is fed up with their earthly loved one attempting to contact them frequently. It can mean they simply can't get through at the time or possibly want their grieving loved one to move on and be happy in this life. It's a very difficult decision for all involved but it can be a case of having to be cruel to be kind sometimes.

So, when someone who never reached old age passes into the afterlife, the feelings of anger and desperation left behind can never be eased by the well-meaning words of anyone. But I believe wholeheartedly what spirit have informed me; that they have simply stepped through the doorway that we will all enter one day and are waiting patiently for their earthly friends and family to join them after we've learned some more lessons in this life. One thing's for sure, they will always be forever young.

Well, as we part our ways now I'd like to thank you for reaching this far in my wee book. If you are Scottish I hope you can appreciate the historical land you live in and if you're not Scottish, then come visit us . . . but remember to bring your wellies as it does rain on occasion!

If you're a believer, then thank you, if you're on the fence, thank you still . . . if you're a sceptic, why did you get this far? Thanks anyway.

Edinburgh, Glasgow, Aberdeen, Dundee, Inverness and indeed all the towns and villages through our wee country have one thing in common; they are all steeped in history, and if you dig deep enough and listen closely enough and keep your eyes peeled, maybe the souls who once lived wherever you are now may still be able to tell their story. Just think; we're only another chapter in that story.

11

THE PSYCHIC TOURIST

There are many people out there who have a deep fascination with the paranormal world and would love to be able to sit in on an overnight paranormal investigation with a group and to do so can occasionally be a thrilling and informative experience. Sometimes, however, modern life – work, family and other commitments – prevent many from having enough free time to be able to dedicate their evenings to any serious exploration of the unknown. And, as I've mentioned in an earlier chapter, to dedicate oneself to searching for spiritual proof shouldn't be taken lightly and takes guts, determination and lots of strong coffee.

However, there is an easier and far less tiring way to come face to face with our country's long dead inhabitants. In every area throughout Scotland there are many historic locations that are spiritually active and can be visited by anyone during the day and, even though there won't be an EMF detector or night-cam in sight, there may still be some activity.

Always remember that spirits aren't only active in the middle of the night – I've seen and sensed many entities in broad daylight too. Any information a psychic receives may even be a bit more accurate during the day because the mind is obviously more alert and there is a lower chance of hallucinations caused by tiredness or the eyes playing tricks in the dark. So, if you can tune your mind in to a location before visiting, you never know what you might pick up there, no matter what time of the day it is. (Go back to chapter nine for a short meditation exercise.)

After some thought, I've made up a wee list here that is in no way exhaustive because, if I was to list every alleged haunted place in this land, it would take up a whole other book. All the places here have been visited by me in my life at one time though, for one reason or another, although never as a real investigation. Some are beautiful and some, I have to say, are downright mingin'. But I've been at them all and can honestly say I've sensed something at each and every site and hopefully you will too. I'd advise anyone who wishes to find out more about our history to check out Historic Scotland or the National Trust for Scotland and lend their support to preserve our cultural heritage.

I've decided to steer away from the numerous alleged haunted pubs, hotels and inns that are dotted throughout the country but they'll be easy enough to find if you look hard enough – as my granny used to say, 'Ye're big enough and ugly enough tae dae it yerself.' And who would argue with that? (I've given some clues in chapter six though.)

I've tried to make sure most of the locations I mention are accessible to the public so get your duffel coat, wellies and hip-flask ready and don't take my word for it . . . go and see for yourself. But please check in advance for the opening times and availability of access of castles etc.

Two of the buildings (hospitals) I've listed don't allow the public to wander around their corridors – unless you are ill or have someone sick to visit of course. But I thought I'd add them for a wee bit of info because they're in close proximity to other locations I've written about and can be viewed from outside. I've also added a few haunted roads just for your info too and I'd strongly advise against sitting at the side of a busy road asking out for communication . . . you might end up joining the spirit world sooner than you think by getting killed. Just travel carefully.

I've tried my best not to divulge too much information to you about the identity of any alleged ghosts and spirits in the places listed – for instance names, dates etc. – because I'm trying not to lead you in anyway. It's better if *you* can walk into a place and see what *you* can pick up yourself. If you really want to find out, there are many books on the shelves that will give you some of the info and many of the staff at locations themselves are able to help if you haven't got a clue. Just remember this is all a wee bit of fun and don't worry if you don't pick anything up at the locations – just enjoy seeing a part of Scotland you've never seen before. But I hope most of you will sense something in some of the places listed. Let's go . . .

First of all, let's travel northwards and visit some places I think will be of interest to historians and ghost hunters alike.

Let's head north and start with a road. The **A9** is the longest running road in Scotland and also has the dubious title of being the second most haunted road in the whole of the UK which makes it Scotland's most haunted. (It was beaten by the M6.) An apparition of a horse and carriage with footmen in powdered wigs has been seen there and someone once reported a sighting of a horseman in Victorian garb galloping around.

Staying on the theme of roads for a moment, there have also been sightings of a ghostly car on the **A87** near Glenshiel which has scared the daylights out of some motorists. This road is also an accident black spot too so could there be a connection? I must say I am so glad the spirit vehicles were nowhere to be seen when I journeyed along those highways a while back.

Thankfully, ghostly vehicles are few and far between on the roads so, to search for some safer paranormal activity, it's a good idea to visit one of the country's many castles. You could take a wee trip to the fantastic **Castle Fraser** in Grampian. Like most good castles worth their salt, there have been sightings of a ghost. This time it is a lady who wears a long black gown and some have even heard the sound of a party going on in the empty hall. I've visited the place and although I saw and heard nothing unusual the day I was there, the residual energy was great and I'd say that there could be some real activity there. I'm just annoyed there was a party going on and I wasn't invited.

In Aberdeenshire, **Crathes Castle** near Banchory is a superb example of a well-preserved Scottish castle. The gardens are an awesome sight to behold but for those interested in the spiritual aspects, there is the sad apparition of a green lady, who has been seen carrying a wee baby in her arms. She is said to be a servant lassie that mysteriously disappeared after falling pregnant to another employee who was fired. Many years later, workmen unearthed skeletons under a hearth and so it's said the hauntings began to get worse. Another reported sighting here is the spirit of a woman in the grounds. It's said she is either a young girl who was murdered by the widowed lady of the house, after winning the heart of her beloved son, or it is possibly the lady herself who it's said dropped dead screaming 'She comes, she comes!' as she pointed to an empty part of the room after being questioned about the girl's death. Maybe you can find out who the apparition is?

When I visited Crathes Castle, I didn't feel any strong paranormal feelings in the grounds or anywhere around the place, but inside, I was lucky enough to sense and briefly see the green lady, although she didn't have the child in her arms.

Not too far away is **Craigievar Castle**, a beautiful and overpowering sight to behold. The castle is seven storeys high and built in the Scottish baronial style. The ceilings are a great piece of artistic workmanship and the whole place is excellently preserved throughout. It's said a ghost of a man haunts the building after he jumped from a high window instead of facing an enemy who was holding a sharp sword in the room. Reported sounds of ghostly footsteps climbing the steps are said to be the poor spirit of the man reliving his final moments before his death.

During my visit I have to say I genuinely felt no malice or malevolence in this fine castle but did sense some children in spirit form and would happily stay in a place as perfect as this.

Moving along, another lady who wears green has been seen in **Dunstaffnage Castle** in Oban, where it's said she can foretell major events for the Campbell clan. Interestingly, an old Scottish legend states that 'Green Ladies' were actually demons who had the body and hooves of a goat underneath their green gowns. I'd say it is just our eyes picking up the most prominent colour from the apparition though.

When I visited there, I felt a serene feeling of calmness and could sense no negativity at all. This is surprising, as the place has been witness to heightened emotional scenes throughout its history which include a beheading and Flora MacDonald being imprisoned there briefly after she helped Prince Charles Edward Stuart escape to France. The castle was seized by Robert the Bruce and it's said it originally held the Stone of Destiny. The place does have an ideal recipe for a haunting but I personally felt at ease. However, quite strangely, on the day I visited, the only apparition I saw was a man with a huge beard in the chapel grounds, dressed in Victorian-style clothing, who stared at me with a quizzical look on his face before disappearing . . . I'm still trying to figure out who he is.

Moving away from castles for a moment, let's travel to the famous – or infamous – **Glencoe**, a scene of tragedy on 13 February 1692 at 5 a.m. when thirty-eight of the MacDonald clan were mercilessly slaughtered by troops who were led by a Captain Campbell. Many more may have died of hypothermia in the cold hills after escaping but the final number of dead is not known. Like most paranormal tales, it's said that on the anniversary of the slaughter some witnesses have been known to hear the cries of the souls of men and women in the valley. One thing's for sure though, the scenery in Glencoe is breathtaking and if you get a chance to sit in the quietude for a moment, there definitely is an eerie atmosphere that enshrouds the place and your imagination can't help but drift back to that fateful morning long ago. Mine did.

Earlier in the book I spoke about my experience of a ghost train as a wee boy. Well, it seems there is a 'regular service' that runs through **Dunphail** in Moray, even though the old Highland Line closed down years ago. Many people have seen the train and some others have even felt the wind and heard the sound of the ghostly engine as it passes by the exact sight where the station once stood and travels along a track that is no longer there.

If you ever get the chance to visit some of the highlands and islands of our wee country you'll be amazed at the history and energy that is engrained into the fabric of the places. Since I was a wee boy I always wanted to visit the standing stones of **Callanish** on the Isle of Lewis. I finally managed to visit some years back and was blown away by the energy and significance of this great location (and great local hospitality). I sat alone one morning and watched the sun rise over the stones, creating shadows on the ground and have to say I left the place feeling uplifted and at peace with the world and would love to go back some day. Local folklore says they were originally giants who refused to be converted to Christianity by St Kieran and were turned to stone as a punishment! I've heard of being 'stoned' but that's a step too far! (Sorry, couldn't resist that one.) It has to be said that the feeling of being at one with nature here is incredible and it brings your senses into touch with life itself.

On the **Isle of Skye** a phantom car is said to zoom around the roads at breakneck speed and, on closer inspection, it seems there is no driver. There have also been reports of kilted troops marching across the area of Harta Corrie at the Bloody Stone, a scene where the McLeod and MacDonald clans fought hundreds of years ago.

I sat there alone as a boy, scoffing away at my wee packed lunch many moons ago and vividly remember hearing male voices shouting and screaming. I couldn't find out where they were coming from at the time as the place was deserted and I thought no more about it. Unaware of the paranormal reports at the time, I disregarded it until a few years back when I heard of the sightings and wondered if I'd heard the spirits of the clansmen battling. I hope so. I don't think I'd have finished my pieces if I'd known then what I know now!

Let's continue our wee trek. Moving down to **Dundee**, the sight of a regular apparition has been witnessed in an unusual location; a modern shopping centre. The **Wellgate Shopping Centre** was built on the site of an old street of the same name and some people have witnessed the apparition of a woman who floats through the place and allegedly causes the creaking that can be heard when the building is empty. I wonder what she makes of the shops there today.

Another area in the city that I was told about a while back and just had to travel up to investigate was **Bell Street Car Park**, where there have been many reports of crying and sobbing when no living person is around. The car park has sadly been built over an ancient graveyard. The place first came to my attention a few years back when a girl emailed and told me that as she was entering her car one afternoon she was positive she felt the sensation of a little hand grabbing hers and this was quickly followed by the sound of a child crying. She searched the deserted area for the source of the crying for a few moments before jumping into her car, terrified. I do think the violation of their graves has disturbed some of the residents there – such a shame.

While in the area, a place that has frequently been called the 'most haunted castle in Scotland' and is well worth travelling to is **Glamis Castle**, the childhood home of Elizabeth Bowes-Lyon, better known as the late Queen Mother. The tales and legends within this place are incredible: for a start there is the sad figure of a grey lady who allegedly haunts the chapel, a ghostly little servant boy and a lady with no tongue who walks the grounds. However, the most famous (or infamous) ghost in Glamis is Earl Beardie, who it's said plays cards with the devil in a secret room for eternity – some witnesses are said to have heard cursing, swearing and the roll of dice echoing through the castle.

This is a fantastic place and must be visited. I didn't meet or see any famous ghosts, but the atmosphere and residual power here are breathtaking.

One of my favourite attractions in the whole country is berthed in the city of Dundee. It is the HM Frigate *Unicorn* which is a perfectly preserved frigate that was originally launched in 1824. Thankfully, at the time of writing, this fine ship is now open to the public. From the moment you step on board you will be able to see what life was like as a naval crew member long ago and soak up the unique atmosphere of the vessel. In recent years, the ship has been an attraction for many people interested in the paranormal due to the amount of reported phenomena that seem to have happened on board, which include ghostly footsteps, objects being thrown and an apparition of a man, dressed in a naval uniform who haunts the decks.

I would say this ship is definitely haunted and would warn anyone who visits to watch out for the mischievous male entity on board. He seems a nice spirit but enjoyed tickling the heads of the people I was with during my visit to the ship. I was really impressed and would definitely advise a visit to this brilliant piece of history to everyone.

OK, let's say cheerio to Dundee and take a wee trek down to the east coast and have a look at some locations I know about in the area. Firstly, let's head into the city of **Edinburgh** and start in the historic yet spooky old town area. I've already mentioned the famous **Mary King's Close** in the book but I guess it's worth another mention. It's located underneath the High Street leading to the castle and as I said already, multiple sightings of apparitions and activity point to something strange definitely going on down there.

Just down the road is another allegedly haunted place that hasn't seen the light of day for hundreds of years – the **Edinburgh Vaults**, hidden under the South Bridge. The vaults are a dark and foreboding place for believer and sceptic alike and as you travel through the dark tunnels it's hard to imagine so many people living here cheek by jowl in the stench and squalor all those years ago with no running water or sanitation. Many heinous crimes were said to have been committed here, including theft and murder, and it's even rumoured that the notorious serial killers, Burke and Hare, prowled the vaults looking for victims who would end up as another anonymous cadaver on the surgeon's table. I've been invited to a few investigations there but sadly have never had the time to go. Like Mary King's Close, I've heard many reports of activity here and when I visited as a tourist, I did sense several presences and watched two other people in the group swear blind they were being pushed by an unknown force – so from my point of view it's definitely haunted and I would love to spend a night there. Both of these underground places are unique and are a must for anyone interested in the darker side of history and the paranormal.

Staying in Edinburgh old town, let's take a wee walk to **Greyfriar's Kirkyard**. This little cemetery is the final resting place of many people, including John Gray, the guardian of 'Bobby', the famous wee dog mentioned earlier in the book. Bobby's wee body is buried nearby his human friend. Also interred in Greyfriars is William McGonnagall, who is widely known as the worst poet in history. The most infamous of the graveyard's dead residents is 'Bluidy' George Mackenzie, whose spirit is blamed for allegedly roughing up the numerous visitors to the place during one of the many haunted tours that operate nightly . . . euch, who can blame him? Can a man no' get a sleep?

I've been at the graveyard a few times in the past and haven't seen a thing. I did feel a sinister presence watching me at the **Covenanter's Prison**, though, many years ago as I sat alone one afternoon (before they kept the gates locked) and although it could've been a case of overactive imagination, I just had to run out of there!

Moving down the **Grassmarket** area, there are many haunted pubs and places in this part of the old town but it's said the ghost of Major Thomas Weir, who was burned to death in 1670 for 'consorting with the devil' still haunts the area, along with disfigured apparitions and ghostly coaches. This was the place for hangings and the slaughtering of animals so, as you will imagine, someone of a sensitive disposition towards these things will pick up many layers of residual energy. It reminds me of one summer evening as I sat with friends outside a pub in the area (and no, I wasn't drunk). I suddenly felt a real sense of fear come over me for no obvious reason and began to hear screaming and could smell the stench of blood – thankfully this only lasted for a few moments and promptly stopped. I was genuinely shaken by the experience but my friends still insisted it was my round at the bar.

No trip to the city would be complete without visiting **Edinburgh Castle**: there have been many alleged sightings of ghosts including a ghostly dog and a headless drummer. The Ministry of Defence recently released a statement saying there had been no official reports of ghosts from on-duty soldiers over the last few decades in their records but still the rumours persist. The castle is an incredible and worthwhile place to visit and explore for ghost hunters, although I have to say, I didn't personally witness anything paranormal during my visits but can say that the residual energy in the place is tremendous and definitely stimulates the senses.

Close by is the **Camera Obscura** on Castle Hill, which has been open for over 150 years and is still a fascinating attraction where you can see a great panoramic view of Edinburgh projected onto a large dish. It's very hard to describe so you'll have to go see it for yourself, along with the other optical illusions they have. It's said the place has been haunted for many years by a male figure. I had never sensed him during my past visits but as I walked up to the castle recently I was quite surprised to see a pretty woman wearing a faded burgundy-coloured dress walking into the Camera Obscura building; she had her dark hair tied up in a bun and wore a wee scarf on her head. At first I have to admit I thought she was one of the many tour guides in period costume that fill the Royal Mile, until I noticed she was completely translucent! This prompted me to pay the place another visit, and I'm glad I did. I didn't come in contact with any of the other reported spirits in the place though, but will say the Camera Obscura is definitely active and feels haunted. Some of the other optical illusions in the place are well worth seeing too and it just shows how the eyes can play tricks. (Remember that, when investigating ghosts.)

When I walked onto the street the lady I'd seen was nowhere to be seen but I am sure she was a past resident of the building and I'd love to see her again. I can't find any records of sightings of a girl in a faded dress of that colour anywhere, but am looking forward to returning soon and maybe then I'll achieve some contact.

It seems every part of Scotland has a haunted road and the **A7** near the village of Stow in Midlothian is very haunted. Many sightings of phantom vehicles have been reported on that road and it's said they have even caused accidents. Over in **East Lothian** there have been some sightings of a ghost bus too. I wonder if it runs on time.

Let's head across the country and visit **Stirling Castle**. This famous landmark has a few ghosts within its walls. A lady has been seen many times and guess what colour her dress is? That's right, green! Yet another 'Green Lady', who it is said could be an attendant of Mary Queen of Scots and who it's said once saved the Queen's life in a fire. Or some say she could be the daughter of a governor of the castle, who threw herself from the battlements onto the rocks below after the death of her true love. Whoever she is it seems she still haunts the place. Stirling Castle also has a 'Pink Lady' who some claim could be Mary Queen of Scots herself and the sound of heavy footsteps has been heard in the Governor's Block coming from an empty room upstairs – sounds like a perfect haunting and merits investigating further.

I was very lucky to have picked up on several spiritual contacts during my last visit but not of Mary, sadly. She seems to be everywhere though and I'd say the place is very haunted and is well worth heading to.

As we travel around the country let's stop off at **New Lanark** on the River Clyde; this place is a perfectly preserved wee village where many people lived and worked hundreds of years ago. It was founded in the year 1786 by David Dale to house his workforce in the cotton mills. The quality of life for the workers was excellent, compared with the general life in the country's workhouses. David's vision was later carried on by his son-in-law, the philanthropist, Robert Owen, who even created the country's first infant school in 1816. In later years the place fell into decay and lay derelict for a time but over the last two decades it has been rejuvenated and is now a major tourist attraction with displays and historical exhibitions, as well as residential property. It has also had its fair share of ghosts and hauntings over the years and still seems active. One story goes that a young man woke up one night to find an apparition of an old woman sitting at his bedroom window, knitting. She turned and stared at the terrified boy, got up and floated through a closed door. Years later his story was validated by another member of the family who had seen the exact same apparition on another occasion. Since then there have been numerous strange experiences by staff and visitors alike and it seems some of the old mill workers definitely want to remain in the place they once inhabited.

I found the residual history to be very powerful in every street and alley and if you are a seeker of spirit or enjoy being transported back in time then you just *have* to walk through the streets of New Lanark.

I think I'll head to my own home town of **Glasgow** now: Edinburgh seems to have all the famous ghosts and spiritual places within its boundaries but old 'Glesga' has its own fair share of hauntings and psychically charged places too, albeit less famous ones. We'll start by walking up the old High Street area and visiting the **Necropolis**, the 'City of the Dead' which is built on a hill just behind the Cathedral. To enter the Necropolis and ascend the steep slopes to the top is a wonderful experience indeed and as you ascend the winding hill you can't help but notice the graves and tombs becoming grander the nearer you get to the top. It seems the rich and mighty from so long ago are buried at the pinnacle of the hill but there are many graves of the less affluent here too. There are an estimated 50,000 people buried here and only 3,500 tombs. William Miller, the poet, who famously wrote the children's rhyme 'Wee Willie Winkie', has a monument dedicated to him here, although his body is actually buried in a family plot in Tollcross Cemetery, further east. I've personally had a strong spiritual experience in the place before (which I've detailed earlier in the book) and I feel attached to the place but, unlike most graveyards, I feel it's highly charged with spiritual activity at certain times. The unique, dark beauty of this place is incredible and has to be seen. Just keep an eye open and you may see one of its old inhabitants.

As you leave the Necropolis gates and cross the 'Bridge of Sighs' (another active area) let's step into **Glasgow Cathedral**. This, along with St Giles, has to be one of my favourite locations in the world to just sit down inside and enjoy the peace, tranquility and residual energy that lie within the ancient walls. The present building has been used as a place of worship for 800 years and has survived the ravages of time and the reformation and is said to stand where Saint Mungo, the patron saint of the city, built his church. Incidentally, big William Wallace (Braveheart) used to meet with his supporter Bishop Wishart in the cathedral on a regular basis, and witches and heretics were executed on the precinct in front of it so there is an unbelievable amount of residual history in the area to explore. Whether you're religious or not, the medieval beauty of this fine place is a must-see for any visitor . . . and just like Edinburgh old town, the whole area around the cathedral is overcrowded with ghosts from the past.

Just next to the cathedral, although not accessible for the public to walk through, is **Glasgow Royal Infirmary**. In this hospital there have been some sightings of a ghostly ward sister by staff and in the oldest part of the building – which lay unused for a long time – there have been many scenes of alleged activity in its corridors. Quite by chance, an old man began to blether to me in a pub on the High Street one afternoon, and he told me some stories about his time working in the hospital as a night shift porter in the '40s and '50s. He went on to say how he had witnessed several apparitions of a stern-looking ward sister who would float through the corridors regularly 'doing her rounds' seemingly oblivious to anyone else around her. He also said there was a grey figure that he'd only seen twice but couldn't tell if it was a man or woman. Whether his stories were exaggerations fuelled by the whisky I bought him, I'll never know, but they do seem to coincide with other sightings I've been told about since. (He did also tell me he was a second cousin of Frank Sinatra.)

Not too far away is a place that no one could exactly describe as a tourist attraction. It's became rather famous though as one of the country's paranormal hot spots and it's been the scene of many sightings of a spirit man who repeatedly jumps to his death. This location is always open to the public because it's the unlikely ghostly setting of a public bridge across the River Clyde. The place is called **Dalmarnock Bridge** and it's here that some unfortunate passers by have seen a man in his thirties, who wears a three-quarter-length coat and dark trousers and stands staring forlornly into the water. They claim he appears to the naked eye as solid as any living person and then within a few seconds he climbs over the side and proceeds to jump into the deep dark murky water of the Clyde . . . however he doesn't even reach the water because he vanishes into thin air! He's allegedly been seen by several passing motorists and pedestrians and the experience has understandably left them upset and confused afterwards.

This is quite a common type of apparition, where a ghost appears to re-enact their final moments in their physical life, perhaps at certain dates, times or anniversaries, sometimes playing back like a 'recording' of the event. The identity of the poor bloke here seems to be a mystery though and hopefully one day someone somewhere will find out who he is. I have to say I've crossed this bridge a few times throughout the years, totally unaware of the story at the time and have never caught a glimpse of him. I've always felt an oppressive atmosphere though at a certain section of the bridge but whether that's intuitive or not I honestly don't know. It is sad that a disturbing scene like this can occur regularly and it would be good if someday the vision would stop and he could rest in peace.

Just along the water is the **St Andrew's Suspension Bridge**, and, although it isn't well known for ghostly activity, when I was a wee boy crossing it with my mother, I saw a filthy old man sitting cross-legged in the middle of the bridge, begging. My mother gave me some coins to give him and when I turned around he was gone! There was absolutely no way he could have stood up and made it off the bridge by foot in the few seconds we had turned away. The bridge was brought to my attention again recently after receiving an email from a guy who lives in the Gorbals area, who told me he's heard loud cursing and swearing in his ear as he reached the centre of the bridge a few times while walking to his work in the morning. He looked all around him and even down at the water and could find nothing and he was sure there wasn't another living soul around at 6.30 a.m. He takes the bus into work now.

At the other side of the city is the **Museum of Transport**, which sits directly across from leafy Kelvingrove Park. The museum displays all kinds of transport through the ages and is a fascinating day out for anyone. In particular, the recreation of a typical Glasgow cobbled street of the 1930s–1940s is fantastic, with its line of typical shops and its own wee cinema and replica of a Glasgow underground station. But at night, when all the visitors have gone home, the building is empty and the lights are turned out, there have been reports of dark apparitions and the sound of ghostly footsteps running through the cobbled streets of the exhibition as well as ghostly screams and noises emanating from around the vehicles.

I've visited the place numerous times and had a very bizarre encounter one afternoon as I sat in the cinema area: I came face to face with a solid apparition of a spirit man in a coat and hat. (His clothes looked as if they were soaked.) A smell of dampness and pipe tobacco filled the air as he sat down a few seats away from me – even though he wasn't smoking. I genuinely thought he was 'alive' because the seat he sat on folded down. I turned to smile and ask him about the rain outside when he simply disappeared. And just like the man others have witnessed at Dalmarnock Bridge, he seemed as real as you or I. I suppose the assorted vehicles that are in the museum may hold strong residual energy and who knows, maybe some of the spiritual owners don't want to be apart from their beloved earthly cars. The Transport Museum is a definite hive of supernatural activity, as well as being a great Glasgow attraction to see and it's well worth finding. In 2009 it will be moving to a new location on Glasgow Harbour – I wonder if the ghosts will follow?

Incidentally, just across the road from the Museum of Transport is the **Western Infirmary**, where it's said that the white ghost of an eminent surgeon who died many years ago, still walks the corridors. The recently refurbished Kelvingrove Art Gallery and Museum which is adjacent also has some strange phenomena reported in the past too.

Moving out of Glasgow, let's go to Ayrshire: just outside Galston there is **Loudoun Castle**. The whole castle which is sadly in ruins today, was built in the early nineteenth century and incorporates a much earlier building within its structure. However, it was gutted by fire in 1941 and has been uninhabited since. Although it's a shell, the building still retains a grand elegance. Years ago there had been reported sightings of a Benevolent Monk, a Grey Lady and a Phantom Piper in Loudoun Castle but it seems the sightings faded over time as daily life in the house ceased on that fateful night. Another interesting fact of this area is that there is a yew tree nearby, said to be over 800 years old, under which it's said the treaty between Scotland and England was prepared, so just imagine the residual energy in this area. The shell of the castle is now surrounded by an excellent theme park and the high energy and hustle and bustle of the place create a unique atmosphere in Loudoun Castle. There was no sign of the ghosts in the grounds while I was there, only residual vibes of benevolence and modern vibes of happiness. Maybe the ghosts of Loudoun Castle prefer to remain hidden within the burned-out ruins of the house these days? A visit here is a great day out.

Another Ayrshire castle that I'd say is well worth going to is **Culzean Castle**, which is still intact and has a few ghosts who allegedly dwell within its confines. This overpowering edifice that stands atop a cliff overlooking the Firth of Clyde, was built in the late eighteenth century and was handed over to the National Trust for Scotland by the Kennedy family in the 1940s, although they asked that the top floor be given to General Eisenhower as a thank you from the people of Scotland for America's help during the war. He gratefully accepted and spent several vacations there enjoying the peace and tranquility of the place, away from the pressure of his office back home. He stayed at the castle even after becoming President of the USA and the suite is still perfect today.

There have been a few sightings of ghosts here, including an unknown young lady ghost seen in a ballroom gown who was seen on the main stair as recently as the early 1970s. Culzean also has its own ghostly piper who some say can be heard when the water is wild and crashing against the rocks below. The story goes that he can also be heard playing when a Kennedy family member is about to get married.

In recent years, the place has been the subject of a good few paranormal investigations by intrepid ghost hunters; such is the interest in this excellent haunted building. While there, I personally found the armoury and the kitchen full of psychic energy and thoroughly enjoyed seeing and communicating with some spirits throughout this great house.

OK, let's head down to the Dumfries area.

On the **A75**, there have been many strange and bizarre reports of apparitions, ranging from entities wandering dangerously across the road dressed in old-fashioned attire only to disappear into thin air, right through to flying creatures, an old woman and weird-looking beasts who all vanish into thin air as they hit the car driven by the poor witnesses. It was reported locally that one ghostly couple walking arm in arm were 'knocked down' by a lorry driver only to disappear when the shaken driver searched the road afterwards.

I wonder, could there be any possibility that some

natural gas leak in the area at the times of the incidents caused the people involved to hallucinate? Another more spiritual theory is that it could be some portal to the spirit world and the witnesses just happen to be driving through it at a very active time in the lunar calendar and it's a case of being in the wrong place at the wrong time. As you can imagine, it's a very difficult location to investigate because of the distinct possibility of being killed by the traffic, so I've only really driven through it in the past. However, I do feel it's a very active road and personally, I'd say the chances of it actually being a portal to the other side are very high. Whatever the reasons for the strange phenomena, just drive carefully.

Many people have emailed me in the past and told me about **Lincluden Collegiate Church**. This once-fine building which stands as a ruin today beside the Cluden Water has had an interesting history, which began as far back as 1160. It has been through the hands of many owners, and even at one stage was used as a quarry. Thankfully now, the ruins are preserved by Historic Scotland. Even though the place has never been on any lists of ghosts and hauntings I know of, two separate eye-witnesses emailed me some years back and said they saw the dark figure of a nun floating through the ruins and it's said to have its very own Green Lady. Incidentally, the church was originally a priory for Benedictine nuns, so that could explain the sightings of a nun I suppose. One of the locals told me that the church had sadly been the target of vandals in recent years – could they have disturbed a female spirit who is there? The Green Lady sightings, however, have been a part of the local folklore for many years and her apparition is said to be linked to

Robert III's daughter, Princess Margaret, who is interred there. So, as you can imagine, yours truly just had to pay the place a visit and see what he could pick up.

While there I did manage to receive direct spirit communication with a young nun and a wee girl around the age of nine. I also picked up on the residual energy of a wee boy who had met an untimely death in the area in the late 1700s but the Green Lady of Lincluden seemed to evade me. Better luck next time I suppose. The place is definitely worth visiting and there's also some good local hospitality close by for thirsty ghost hunters too.

OK, pack yer bags and follow me. On the banks of the River Tweed are the ruins of **Dryburgh Abbey**. The quiet location of this abbey and the surrounding gardens really help to relax the mind and I personally found it extremely easy to meditate here. This fine and serene location where the physical remains of Sir Walter Scott and Field Marshall Haig are interred nearby, has had its share of terrible events throughout its turbulent history. It's said that Edward II's army, retreating back to England in 1322, ordered it to be razed to the ground after hearing the bells played in celebration of his defeat. After being rebuilt, another raid in the 1500s by a few hundred English troops completely destroyed the abbey and the nearby town of Dryburgh, thereby ending any inhabitation within the abbey and it has lain empty since.

A local story tells of a lady in a house that once stood nearby, who fell in love with a monk at the abbey and when their wee affair was discovered the poor bloke was hanged in full view of her window. It's said that in her intense shock and grief she then walked onto the bridge, threw herself into the river and is now the unnamed Grey Lady who has been seen on that same bridge and surrounding area many times. There have also been sightings of monks in the actual abbey grounds and some witnesses have even heard the sound of male voices chanting within the ruins on occasion.

I visited the location unofficially one fine summer afternoon with investigator Tom M and I was instantly taken aback by the large numbers of benevolent spirit monks who still reside there. I've honestly never seen so many entities in one place. I counted at least fifteen benevolent spirits throughout the grounds but none of them would – or could – communicate with me. They seemed to ignore me. Even though the weather that afternoon was warm and sunny, Tom M and I felt some extreme cold areas in the place but we both put that down to the close proximity to the water and the position of the remains. However, the areas actually felt ice cold even though they were in direct sunlight – and I did sense a group of spirit energies in one icy spot who were standing in a perfectly formed circle and chanting. It was a strange sight to see.

Dryburgh Abbey and the area that surrounds it is genuinely one of the calmest and most enjoyable locations I've been to as a visitor and like the other places listed in this chapter, very active.

Well, I think that wee journey should keep you busy for a few weekends. If you do decide to visit the same places I've visited, I really hope you pick up some psychic vibes and maybe witness some people who are still there from the past. If you don't pick a thing up, then I hope you enjoy visiting different parts of this great land anyway and please show your support for every historic location we have so that one day our own descendents can appreciate them too. I'm sure they won't be paying to see any of the modern office blocks that stand today.

I've been to literally hundreds of spiritual places throughout Scotland and plan to visit them all one day, but the ones here are worth investigating as a tourist and that's why they're listed here.

This ancient country has an intense character and spiritual energy embedded into every stone and piece of earth in its towns, cities and countryside that genuinely make it a goldmine for paranormal investigators and historians. As I said at the start of the book, our past has been filled with love, hate, jealousy, anger and bloodshed so each piece of earth we stand on and each building we enter is filled with layers of powerful energy from the past, which is being added to by the present occupiers of this world.

Who knows, maybe one day in a few hundred years someone with heightened senses will be standing on the very same piece of ground we are on right now and they may pick up on any residual energy that we've left behind and receive information about us. Oh dear, we'd better start behaving.

Whoever you are and whatever your beliefs, take care on your journey through your physical life and, as some say here in Scotland, 'Lang May Yer Lum Reek!'